Did Trojans Use Trojans?

A Trip Inside the Corner Drugstore

VINCE STATEN

A FIRESIDE BOOK
PUBLISHED BY SIMON & SCHUSTER
NEW YORK LONDON TORONTO SYDNEY SINGAPORE

FIRESIDE
Rockefeller Center
1230 Avenue of the Americas
New York, NY 10020

First Fireside Edition 2000
FIRESIDE and colophon are registered trademarks
of Simon & Schuster, Inc.

Designed by Deirdre C. Amthor
Manufactured in the United States of America
10 9 8 7 6 5 4 3 2 1

The Library of Congress has cataloged the Simon & Schuster edition as follows:
Staten, Vince, date.
    Do pharmacists sell farms?: a trip inside the corner drugstore./
Vince Staten.
        p.   cm.
    1. Staten, Vince, date.   2. Businessmen—United States—Biography.
3. Drugstores—United States—History.   4. Pharmaceutical industry—
United States—History.   I. Title.
    HD9666.95.S83A3   1998
    381'.45615'092—dc21
    [B]   98-6155
                                                                        CIP

ISBN 0-684-83485-5
       0-684-85433-3 (Pbk)
Previously published as *Do Pharmacists Sell Farms?*

Trojans is a registered trademark of Carter-Wallace Inc. This book is not affiliated with
or authorized by Carter-Wallace Inc.

Acknowledgments

A few years ago I was in Milledgeville, Georgia, for the annual running of the bulls—no, that wasn't Milledgeville. Anyway, I was in Milledgeville and had occasion to stop by the local bookstore. Milledgeville, for those who are not fans of Christ-haunted, Southern Gothic burlesques, is the hometown of Flannery O'Connor. They sell her works at that bookstore, where I found them shelved under "Local Authors." It was something O'Connor, with her wonderfully wry sense of humor, would have appreciated. The greatest of Southern short story writers is, in her hometown, a "local author."

Last time I was in my hometown I checked my friendly neighborhood Bookland, my favorite east Tennessee bookstore, and found my last book, *Did Monkeys Invent the Monkey Wrench? Hardware Stores and Hardware Stories,* filed between a dictionary and a thesaurus. My memoir of growing up in a hardware family is a reference book.

My book *Can You Trust a Tomato in January?,* a history of grocery stores and grocery store food, is invariably sandwiched among the cookbooks. I can only wonder where this book will wind up on the bookstore shelves. I hope you didn't buy it thinking it might be a guide to agricultural real estate.

It's not an easy book to categorize.

It may end up among the health-care books, even though there isn't a single sentence of health advice. I'm not a physician and I haven't played one on TV, so I'm really not qualified to tell anyone what to take and when to take it. It could find a home in the drug-reference section, although it's not a guide to the use of drugs—prescription, over-the-counter, recreational, whatever.

So what is it? I tell people it's a social history of drugstores and drugstore products. If you've ever stood in line cradling your latest drugstore purchase—whether a box of Ex-Lax, a package of condoms or a copy of *True Confessions* magazine—and wondered how we came to buying laxatives, rubbers or confession magazines, then this is the book for you.

So what section should it be in in the bookstore? How about the best-seller shelf?

I was aided in my search for these answers by a number of friends, students, relatives and general hangers-on.

Jenny Allen conducted much of the corner drug survey with panache and aplomb, plus she got a lot of reluctant old pharmacists to talk. Shirl Ryan is a researcher extraordinaire—she doubled up behind me on a number of topics and came up with even more material. Kathy Furrow had fun and got class credit for her research contributions. John McDonald, a funny guy in his own write, gave me the Preparation H punch line.

My wife and my kids put up with an awful lot when I write a book; they should at least get a little applause at the end of it all. So let's all put our hands together and thank them. And get on to the next book—yours to read, mine to write.

To all my teachers, especially the ones I never forgot: Miss Wilkinson, Miss Tipton, Mrs. Lewis, Mrs. Larkin, and, best of all, Mrs. Pridemore

Contents

1
Down at the Old Corner Drug: Elbowing My Way In

There we are on page 97 of my high school yearbook: Cynthia Perry and Dale Hickam, Jean Rogers and Danny Pomeroy, Steve Lambert and Mary McAlpine, and my elbow, just creeping into the frame. We were posing for the yearbook photographer at the local teen hangout, the soda fountain of Armour's Drugs. Armour's was just two blocks from school. An easy walk, except that no one walked. We drove. We were seniors.

Armour's Drugs was the place to see and be seen, to nurse a cherry Coke for an hour while you kept your eye on the front door, hoping that SHE—whoever she was this week—would stroll in. And also hoping that SHE wouldn't be with some other boy. And maybe she would sit down next to you and you could call out to Mabel to get you another straw and you two could sit there, sharing a cherry Coke, like a picture out of *The Saturday Evening Post*.

Maybe that's why I got cut out of the picture that long-ago day. I wasn't with someone; I was watching for HER.

That was the drugstore of my youth. A social center for teenagers, and a community center for adults. While we sat around posing for that photo perhaps a dozen moms came in, some to pick up prescriptions, others to pick up what are today grocery items: toothpaste, shampoo, aspirin. They would stop and talk with old Doc Armour, because he was the master of ceremonies of the drugstore. He did more than dispense drugs from his perch in the back of the store. He also dispensed gossip and advice. He knew it all—who was sick, who was well, who was in the hospital, who was back at home. There was always a new patent medicine to cure the common cold, a new ointment for backaches and a new powder for itches. Maybe he was practicing medicine without a license, but that's what family pharmacists did in the sixties.

Drugs were Doc Armour's main business. That was, after all, his middle name: Armour's *Drug* Store. Back then, no one just ran into the drugstore, grabbed up their stuff and ran right out. The drugstore was a place to linger, to catch up.

Even eat. I had many a drugstore lunch in my youth. When my mother and I would "go to town" (a weekly event, even though we only lived five hundred feet outside the city limits), we'd always have lunch at Freel's Drug, home of the best grilled cheese sandwich in America.

The drugstore was the cracker barrel of the city.

Armour's Drugs was the place where my crowd congregated after school. But by the time we got around to posing for the yearbook photo, Armour's was on its way out as the place to see and be seen. Heck, it closed at six o'clock.

There was this new place up the road, right across the street from my father's hardware store, as a matter of fact, and this new place stayed open well into the night. There was no counter and no booths and no place to sit except on the hood of your car, but by 1965 McDonald's was well on its way to supplanting the corner drug as the gathering spot of our culture.

Corner Drug.

No name says "small town" like Corner Drug. No name evokes memories of soda fountains and Saturday afternoons like Corner Drug.

Corner Drug is where Grandma met Grandpa, where Mom bought her first home permanent and Dad his first rubber (that's condom, to you kids). It was once a staple of every downtown, the place where mothers met in the morning to gossip, where businessmen lunched and cut deals, where teenagers crowded in after school for a soda and a smile.

My godmother, who got married in 1934, celebrated with a wedding dinner at the soda fountain of Bunting's Drugs in Bristol, Virginia. "We got three hot dogs for a dime. He ate two and I ate one."

But downtown corners have lost their luster, replaced by malls, and Corner Drug stores have been snapped up by Rite-Aid and Revco, who may give the old Corner Drugs a big-time name, but they rob the places of their identities.

There are only seventy-one drugstores named Corner Drug remaining, according to my search of business phone directory listings. There's no way of knowing how many there once were, but every town had one.

A few of the remaining Corner Drugs have moved away from the corner to a strip center, retaining their old name if not their old location. But most have held on to that coveted downtown corner, even as downtown has changed. As the owner of Corner Drugs in Llano, Texas, put it, "We've been here forever."

I surveyed the surviving members of the Corner Drug fraternity to find out how they've changed and how they've remained the same.

Of the seventy-one drug stores named Corner Drug, fifty-one agreed to answer a few questions. (Isn't it good to know that fully 28 percent of all Corner Drug store owners are suspicious of someone who calls on the phone claiming to be writing a book about drugstores?)

Changing times and changing fashions have hurt the soda fountain business. In 1948, 60 percent of America's drugstores had working soda fountains, according to that year's edition of *Remington's Practice of Pharmacy*. Only 20 percent of today's Corner Drugs—ten stores—have soda fountains. And only four of those ten serve lunch. One serves ice cream only; the others offer fountain service. In a nod to modern times, two other Corner Drug stores have coffee bars. Photo finishing, a drugstore staple for a century, has fared better: 70 percent of Corner Drugs still offer that old drug store standby.

The day of the family-owned pharmacy isn't over either. But the big corporations have made an attempt to corner the Corner Drug market—they now own 40 percent of the drugstores I surveyed.

How old are Corner Drugs? They are as old as God and as new as Zantac 75. Corner Drug in Sigourney, Iowa, was founded in 1875, the year *before* Rutherford B. Hayes was voted into office. (The state was only twenty-nine years old at the time.) One encouraging sign about the future of Corner Drugs is that they are still being built in the nineties. Corner Drug of Buffalo, Missouri, opened in 1991, and the Corner Drug Store at 451 Third Avenue in New York City opened in 1992. The average

age of these Corner Drugs is sixty-seven (founded in 1930). If you're into math, the median age is sixty-nine.

Most Corner Drug stores are legitimate corner drugstores, located on the corner of two intersecting streets in the downtown area. But one—Corner Drug of Durant, Oklahoma—is located "in" a corner. Three used to be on corners, but have moved. Corner Drug in Lake City, Tennessee, used to be on the corner, but other businesses in the east Tennessee town have built up around it and now it is in the middle of the block.

Corner Drug of Cattaraugus, New York, is on a dangerous corner by a steep hill, and the store has been hit by cars several times. One druggist—that guy at Corner Drug in Llano, Texas—felt compelled to tell us that his store had only been on a corner for ninety-nine years. It didn't move to the corner until 1898, five years after the store's founding. The Corner Drug in Driggs, Idaho, gets our nod as best source for one-stop shopping: It's called Corner Drug & Hardware.

Whether the store is an old-timer or a newborn, the folks at Corner Drug have some stories to tell. That's because in most places the local pharmacist is much more approachable than the doctor. He'll even pick up the phone.

At Corner Drug in Columbus, Texas, they still laugh about the woman who thought "free delivery" meant that she didn't have to pay when they delivered it to her house.

A woman called Corner Drug in Lander, Wyoming, panicked that her children had cooked her birth control pills in the toaster. She said they were a little brown and wondered if they were still good. (They were.)

The ladies at Corner Drug in Bethany, Missouri, were taken aback the day an old guy forgot he was in public and dropped his pants right there in the store so he could tuck in his shirt.

It's been thirty years, but they still chuckle about the lady who called Corner Drug Store in Blacksburg, Virginia, to inform the pharmacist that she had taken her medicine and chased it with wine, apparently making it explode in her stomach, causing smoke to come out of her mouth. She was not hurt, she explained, but she just wanted them to know.

Corner Drug Store in Glenwood, Minnesota, is in Garrison Keillor country, so they should have known better when the Norwegian fellow asked for a "urinal." They finally figured out what he was saying—he wanted a "Journal," a *Milwaukee Journal*. Pharmacists at that store still go the extra mile. One night, the pharmacist got a panicked call at home from a man with a screaming baby in the background. He drove ten miles on his snowmobile in a BLIZZARD only to find that the guy who called just wanted to buy a pacifier.

There was a shoot-out in 1932 in the Corner Drug Store of Madill, Oklahoma. The sheriff and a deputy shot and killed each other. Folks there today like to note that both men were "peace" officers.

A robbery at Corner Drug Store in Carlsbad, New Mexico, in 1995 turned comical when the pharmacist, who had just been held up, ran out of the front of the store to see which way the robber was headed. He saw the thief pedaling down the street on a bicycle. The pharmacist jumped in his car and chased the guy while calling the police on his cellular phone. The robber was soon apprehended.

The regulars at Corner Drug Store in Seal Beach, California, were worried about the impending arrival of the comet Kahoutek back in the seventies, so when the store's front window suddenly shattered on the day the comet was to pass by, everyone was petrified. It turned out that it was an old lady who thought her car was in reverse and crashed into the store.

Every pharmacist, it seems, has a story about an ignorant customer. At the Corner Drug Store in Bridgeton, Missouri, they have two such stories. In one, a lady calls to complain that her child's medication is making his ear red. It turns out that the prescription was for an oral liquid and she was pouring it directly into the kid's infected ear. In the other story someone calls the pharmacy complaining that his suppository is a little "rough" going in. The pharmacist asks, "Did you remove the foil?" to which the customer replies, "You're supposed to remove the foil?"

My favorite Corner Drug story was told to me by a Mississippi druggist. It seems the ballplayer Dizzy Dean was a regular at his store. On this particular steamy south Mississippi day, Ol' Diz limped in and asked the clerk for jock itch powder. "Sir, could you walk this way?" the clerk asked, leading him to the proper aisle, to which Diz replied, "If I could walk that way, I wouldn't need the powder."

The Corner Drug Store in Pickens, South Carolina, claims to be America's only haunted drugstore. Numerous times, people in the back bathroom have heard someone walk by with heavy shoes, but when they check, no one is there. The owner thinks the ghost may have come from an old house that was there before the drugstore. He has checked pipes and other possible sources of the noise and found no other causes. So he has come to accept that it's a ghost. Maybe it's the ghost of Miss Ellie, the friendly pharmacist of *The Andy Griffith Show.* Pickens is down there not far from Mayberry territory.

One of the most amazing corner drugstore stories comes from F. E. Robinson's Drug Store in Dayton, Tennessee. It was a gorgeous spring day in 1925—the dogwoods were in bloom and the robins were in song—when a few of the regulars gathered by the soda fountain at Robinson's. It was the usual chatter: a little politics, a little gossip, a little hashing over the dispatches in the newspaper. One of the regulars was George Rappelyea, who did as much hanging out as he did working, due to his depleted economic situation. He was in the process of closing down his father-in-law's bankrupt coal mine.

One dispatch in the *Chattanooga Daily Times* caught Rappelyea's eye. The Tennessee state legislature had passed a law, the Butler Act, that forbade the teaching of evolution in the public schools. The American Civil Liberties Union was appalled at this new challenge to academic freedom, and a spokesperson from the New York office told the *Daily Times* that it was ready to fund a challenge to the law. That piqued Rappelyea's interest. A big trial like that might just be what sleepy little Dayton needed. Think of all the attention the town would get, all the folks who would crowd in.

Rappelyea mentioned his idea to his Coke-swigging buddies Walter White, the superintendent of Rhea County Schools, and Sue Hicks, a gentleman lawyer with an unlikely first name. Druggist Frank Robinson, who was also the town's leading textbook merchant, wandered over and offered his support of the idea. Hicks was interested. Only White, who would bear the brunt of any courtroom action, was hesitant. Rappelyea turned it into a bet: "As it is, the law is not enforced. If you win, it will be enforced. If I win, the law will be repealed." White couldn't resist a sporting proposition. And so the most famous trial of the twentieth century (ask your history professor) was born: The Scopes monkey trial didn't begin in a classroom. It began in a drugstore.

Only after Rappelyea and his soda fountain buddies had settled on a plan did they find a victim—John Thomas Scopes, a twenty-four-year-old football coach and science teacher. In all likelihood Scopes never taught a sentence of evolutionary theory to Dayton High School students. He taught biology for only two weeks, filling in for the ailing regular teacher. When questioned that day in May 1925, he wasn't sure what he had covered in his ten days of teaching biology: "We reviewed for final exams, as best I remember." But his name is in the history books, and the name F. E. Robinson's Drug Store should be there alongside it.

The Scopes monkey trial isn't the only thing to have started in a drugstore over the years; there's also Lana Turner's career, more than a few romances, and even this book.

Let's take a look at Simon's Prospect Apothecary in Prospect, Kentucky. My drugstore.

Last time I was in, pharmacist Alan Simon was doling pills into a prescription bottle without looking at the prescription, without looking at the big bottle of pills he got off the shelf and only glancing at the measuring slate or the pill bottle with the little safety cap that he was filling. He was talking the entire time about a court battle our city has been waging against a developer who wants to build a giant shopping center with a super grocery store, five restaurants and assorted other modern franchise marvels. Prospect won the latest round in what is now an eight-year battle. "Oh, he'll appeal," Simon said nonchalantly.

"And he'll probably win the next round. Circuit court has never been friendly to us."

You'd think Simon was the mayor of Prospect if you just stood around listening. He isn't, but he might as well be. There isn't anything that happens in town that he doesn't know about: the break-in at the restaurant, the fatality on the bypass, or even the Charles Manson look-alike who has been wandering the streets of town for the last two days. "He's harmless. I admit, he'd spook me if I was out alone at night. But he's a friendly fellow, some LSD burnout from up in Michigan who somehow hitchhiked his way south and landed here. They'll probably put him on the bus home tomorrow."

By all rights, Simon's Apothecary should have gone under years ago. It sits in the shadow of a giant Rite-Aid chain drugstore that stays open twenty-four hours. Where Rite-Aid stocks eighty-seven varieties of painkillers, from Doan's Pills to Stanback Pain Relief Powders to the standard garden varieties of Tylenol, Bayer, Advil and Anacin, Simon's carries a few bottles of Tylenol and a few bottles of Bayer. That's bottles, not varieties.

Simon doesn't sell choice. He doesn't compete on price or selection. He sells service and himself.

He's the town druggist and Simon's Apothecary is the corner drugstore, even if it's not on a corner. Folks in Prospect couldn't even tell you the name of the druggist at Rite-Aid. "It's some college kid they hired right off the graduation platform," jokes Simon. "He'll be here ten months and then off to seek his fortune. 'Cause it's for sure he's not going to get it from Rite-Aid."

Pills and politics are serious business for Simon. It's more than Prospect that's fighting the developer. Simon himself has been slapped with a so-called SLAP suit—Slander and Libel

Against Plaintiff—charging that he has violated the developer's civil rights. "I had to hire a lawyer, but my insurance will cover it. It's just intimidation. He doesn't like the idea of some guy in a corner drug telling people what he's trying to do."

But much as I like Alan and much as I like sitting in his store soaking it all in, it's not a daily stop on my agenda. Drugstores just aren't the integral part of our lives they once were. Oh, they are still important places. The average family visits the drugstore sixteen times a year, more than once a month. That pales next to the grocery store, where Americans shop eighty-six times a year, but it's not far behind mass merchants. The average American visits the Wal-Mart or one of its competitors more than twenty-eight times a year.

The prime customers at drugstores, as you might suspect, are older folks. Retirees generate 39.5 percent of a drugstore's business.

Drugstores' main competitors are the supermarkets and the discount stores, and in many areas, the drugstores have lost out. But they are still the market of choice for twenty-nine major items, including cosmetics, cold and sinus tablets, hair coloring, hand and body lotion, laxatives, suntan products, nasal spray and contraceptives.

The number-one product in the drugstore is . . . drum roll . . . Tylenol, with $329.4 million in drugstore sales in 1995. Revlon cosmetics are second with $254.8 million. Third place goes to Cover Girl cosmetics with $193.7 million. Maybelline cosmetics rank fourth with $175.1 million in sales.

I've been fascinated by drugstores since my elbow made it into the high school yearbook. That's what this book is about: The drugstore in all its many incarnations, pharmacy and apothecary, drugstore and general store, prescription center and community center, soda fountain and social hub. It's a book about what's inside the corner drug, from the products to the people.

And it's about that time when the drugstore was the most important store in town. Because for many towns, it still is.

At the turn of the century, the old general store used to advertise that it could take care of you from "cradle to grave." They sold cradles and they sold caskets. By the time of my youth, the 1950s and '60s, general stores were gone. Drugstores had taken over many of their functions. And if the drugstore couldn't actually do the cradle-to-grave bit (I've never seen a casket in a drugstore, and I'm sure it would frighten off a goodly portion of the clientele), the drugstore could handle all your needs from head to toe. Aspirin for the headache, powder for foot itch; Pepto-Bismol for an upset stomach, a soda fountain burger for an empty one.

And that's how this book is organized, to take you through the drugstore, to examine all the products you use from head to toe. The drugstore even has something for that elbow of mine. But first let's take a look at the history of the drugstore.

2
The History of the Drugstore:
Or, as Much as You'll Ever Need to Know

It was a cinch to be a druggist in Grandpa's day. A jug of creosote, a bottle of wintergreen, a couple of mustard plasters, a jar of leeches and you were in business. But now, oh, brother. Now a druggist must run a combination department store, hospital, book nook, candy kitchen, post office and short-order restaurant. But he still must handle a few leeches. And here's one of them, with his wife, in Kremer's Drug Store as we meet Fibber McGee and Molly.

—Announcer introduction to an episode
of the forties radio show *Fibber McGee and Molly*

The first pharmacist probably didn't wear a little white coat with a mortar and pestle on the pocket. And he probably didn't perch on a little elevated platform above the rest of the pharmacy. He probably wore deer antlers and a skin cloak and jumped up and down and shouted nonsense syllables as he filled his patient's prescription. And he probably went by the name *medicine man* or *shaman.*

The first image that we have of a pharmacist was painted

some 14,000 years ago by a Magdalenian cave dweller in the
Les Trois Freres cave in Ariege in southwest France. It shows a
little stick figure wearing a white smock and standing in front of
a mortar and pestle. I'm sorry, that's a picture of Mr. Kremer at
Kremer's Drug Store on *Fibber McGee and Molly*. The first
pharmacist is pictured with deer antlers.

This early pharmacist wasn't really a pharmacist at all.
Shaman really is the closer term. In ancient societies, disease
and infirmity were blamed on evil spirits. So a cure was simple:
just figure out which evil spirit had invaded and why and then
offer him a virgin. Or find some way to drive the spirit out.

The first known prescription dates to 2100 B.C. and ancient
Mesopotamia. It was written on a clay tablet in Sumerian and
advised: "Pulverize [the bark of] the apple tree and the moon
plant; infuse it with kushumma wine; let tree oil and hot cedar
be spread over it." There's no mention, but based on what we
know today, I think we can assume it was to be taken three
times a day. Actually, that clay tablet listed formulas for making
about thirty other simple drugs, from the one above, for relief of
pain, to a simple emetic.

The most important early pharmaceutical prescriptions are
found in the Ebers papyrus—no, not the Siskel and Ebert papyrus with a thumbs up or thumbs down on each formula. It
dates from 1500 B.C. and is named for Georg Ebers, the German
Egyptologist who purchased it in 1872 and made its contents
public. This Egyptian document lists 811 drug formulas using
materials from the vegetable, animal and mineral kingdoms.

Here is the formula "to expel diseases in the belly": "Cumin
½ ro, goose fat 4 ro, are boiled, strained and taken."

The Ebers papyrus proves that constipation is not a modern

TV commercial–created affliction. The papers contain this formula "to open the bowels": "Milk 25 ro, sycamore fruit 8 ro, honey 8 ro, are boiled, strained and taken for four days." We don't know what a "ro" was, but we can be pretty sure it was a very small unit of measurement—otherwise the patient would have had serious problems getting it down.

The drug formulas were important to those ancient healers, but more important were the words spoken with their use, the magic spells. Here's the Ebers papyrus "Recital on Drinking a Remedy," to be spoken to the patient as he slurped that cumin-flavored goose-fat mush:

> Here is the great remedy. Come thou who expellest evil things in this my stomach and drives them out from these limbs. Horus and Seth have been conducted to the big palace at Heliopolis where they consulted over the connection between Seth's testicles with Horus, and Horus shall get well like one who is on earth. He who drinks this shall be cured like these gods who are above . . .
> These words should be said when drinking a remedy. Really excellent, proven many times.

The connection between Seth's testicles and Horus's disease isn't quite as clear today as it was must have been a few thousand years ago, but as the scribe attests, this testicular plea worked for him.

Drugs were just a part of the overall magic that was used in ancient times to heal. Hey, it must have worked at least occasionally, or else these recipes wouldn't have been handed down from generation to generation for a thousand years.

In the years before Christ, there were no pharmacies, although in the Babylonian period there was this one particular street in Sippur where drug sellers plied their trade. There were no pharmacies because there were not yet pharmacists. But we were getting there.

Egyptians had broken down the drug-dispensing role into three jobs: those who collected the materials, those who prepared the drugs and those who took care of the drugs. And there was a special room in the temple where drugs were prepared, the *asi-t*.

So we are closer to the pharmacy era.

Hippocrates is often called the father of modern medicine, which, by extension, would make him the father of modern pharmacy. He rejected the antler-and-skin-cloak magical healing school, preferring a rational, empirical approach to healing. But since he was *not* the father of modern scientific research, his ideas were based on nothing more than theories. And he had some doozies. He believed that there were four bodily fluids, called humors, and they had to be kept in harmony. As you may know, the four were blood, phlegm, yellow bile and black bile, and their properties were, respectively, hot, cold, moist and dry. According to Dr. Hippocrates, you cured by opposites. Phlegm, for instance, meant you were cold and needed heat. His preferred healing methods were bleeding, scarring, blistering, cupping and leeching. Pretty pagan, but it was an advancement over the antler man in the skin cloak screaming gibberish in your ear.

Hippocrates had his pill cabinet—diuretics, laxatives, emetics and expectorants—which he used liberally. His patients were urged to puke, poop, pee and spit to get those humors back into balance. He would get your body back in harmony if it killed him . . . or you.

Hippocrates's methods had some success—they must have, because his theories prevailed for two thousand years. But he didn't have a pharmacy.

People in other civilizations, however, were working hard to invent the pharmacy. A major step forward came from another Greek, the writer Pedanius Dioscorides. He assembled the first pharmaceutical guide, *De Materia medica,* which listed 837 drugs, including some 600 from plants, 35 from animal products and 90 from minerals. It was a prodigious effort and worth every minute of it because it would be *the* pharmaceutical authority for a millennium and a half—1,600 years. Unfortunately for Dioscorides, his copyright was only for fifty-eight years.

It was from these Greeks that we got the word *pharmacy,* if not the pharmacy itself. *Pharmacy* is generally credited to the Greek word *pharmakon,* meaning "remedy."

The Romans—next up in the great march forward to modern civilization—made their own contributions to the development of the pharmacy. The Roman physician Galen created a classification system for drugs, categorizing them by their effects. He counted three groups: the simples, which he defined as having one quality, either cold, hot, dry or moist; the composites, which had more than one quality; and the entities, which had a specific action. He listed 473 drugs in his writings, the most famous 3 being *hiera picra, terra sigillata* and theriaca. *Hiera picra,* a mixture of aloes, spices and herbs in honey, was still in wide use at the beginning of the twentieth century and was said to be the oldest pharmaceutical compound.

Galen prepared his own drugs and kept them in wooden boxes in a storeroom. The Greek word for this storeroom was *apotheca*, and thus our word *apothecary*. And Galen's name lives on today: vegetable-based drugs that involve no real chemical changes are called "galenicals," while their testing and preparation is called "galenics." One of his concoctions lives on, too—he invented cold cream.

The people who really got the ball rolling for the pharmacy, though, were the Arabs. They were the first to introduce a professional literature to pharmaceuticals. In the ninth century A.D., Sabur ibn-Sahl compiled a list of formularies—recipes for preparing drugs—called *al-Aqrabadhin al-Kabir*.

In the eleventh century, the Persian philosopher and physician ibn-Sina, also known as Avicenna, united all medical knowledge of the time in a five-volume *Canon medicinae*. The second volume dealt exclusively with simple drugs, and the fourth with compounds. The *Canon* was translated into Latin in the thirteenth century, and when Guttenberg and his boys got the printing presses going, it was one of the first books published. It was sold throughout Europe and used well into the eighteenth century. In addition to his writings, Avicenna was the first to gild and silver pills, making them easier, if more expensive, to swallow. HMOs would have hated him.

Another Arab contribution to the development of the drugstore was the concept of dosage. Before dosage, the infirm just swallowed whatever was offered. And swallowed and swallowed and swallowed.

The Arabs were also the first to mask medicine's bitter taste, combining their drugs with syrups, confections and juleps, especially those made from sugar and honey. St. Joseph's orange-flavored aspirin for children is a direct descendant of those sugar-coated Arab medicines.

The pharmacist was considered such an important member of the Arab community that there was even a code of ethics adopted in thirteenth-century Cairo. It was called the *Minhaj* (The Handbook), and it provided that pharmacies should be clean and well stocked, with an inventory monitoring system to ensure that decaying products were replaced. The pharmacist was instructed to keep his profits moderate and "to have deep religious convictions, consideration for the poor and needy, a sense of responsibility and be careful and God-fearing." He was also to be friendly, honest, thoughtful, slow to anger, modest and patient. Sounds more like a saint than a druggist.

In addition, the Arabs were the first to license pharmacists; in the ninth century, qualified pharmacists were given licenses to operate near army camps, setting them apart from street vendors.

And here's the biggie: they were the first to have a permanent building for the dispensing of medicine. This first pharmacy shop opened in Baghdad around A.D. 775 and was called *dakakin al-sayadilah,* which is Arabic for "three pharmacists, no waiting." The idea of a drug dispensary in one permanent location was such a good idea that it soon spread all over the civilized world.

It spread—I didn't say it was profitable. If pharmacists today think managed health care is siphoning away their profits, they should have seen pharmacists in fourteenth-century Italy. It was so bad that pharmacists also served as undertakers, just so they could make enough money to get by.

Pharmacists still weren't wearing those little white coats, but they were getting closer. The Magna Carta of pharmacy consisted of the *Constitutiones* issued by Holy Roman Emperor Frederick II between 1231 and 1240. These decrees regulated the medical profession and separated it from pharmacy for the first time in the Western world.

Nevertheless, pharmacists didn't have the respect that they would one day enjoy. In fourteenth-century London, pharmacists were in the same guild as grocers, pepper makers and spice makers.

But things were starting to change. Hippocrates's theories were finally challenged in the sixteenth century by a Swiss physician who wrote under name Paracelsus. He rejected the humor–harmony equation, postulating instead three principles of the human body: combustibility (the sulfur principle); liquidity and volatility (the mercury principle); and stability and solidity (the salt principle). Disease was not an imbalance of humors, he wrote, but a localized abnormality, a chemical problem to be treated chemically. And, for him, like cured like. Finally there was a medical basis for the mixing of chemical formulas. Even if the mixers were still on the same social plane as grocers.

That would soon change. In 1614, Gideon Delaune, apothecary to Queen Anne of Denmark, petitioned Anne's husband, James I of England, to give apothecaries their own guild. Sir Francis Bacon, chief legal advisor to the king, agreed: "Grocers are but merchants, the business of an Apothecary is a Mistery."

The first pharmacy shops opened in America at about this time. Records have survived of a pharmacy shop operating in Boston in 1646 and another in New York in 1653.

Actually, these early pharmacies—in America and elsewhere—were more often called apothecaries. Then came Molière. The French satirist noticed that one of the chief duties of the French *apothicaire*—druggist—was the administration of enemas. He made fun of this practice in his play *Le malade imaginaire* and in the process made *apothicaires* the laughing-stocks of the nation.

The French pharmacists were so shamed that they dropped the name *apothicaire,* the name Molière satirized, and became *pharmacien.* I'll bet your local pharmacist doesn't know it was the enema that made him a pharmacist. I'll also bet he's pretty glad the administration of enemas is no longer in the pharmacist's bag.

Most drugs of the seventeenth and eighteenth centuries were liquids or powders. Then, in 1834, two Frenchmen, F. A. B. Mothes and J. G. A. Dublanc (remember those names; they'll be on the test), invented the soft gelatin capsule. Three years later a hard version of the capsule was patented in England. The capsule, as envisioned by Mothes and Dublanc, had two purposes: to mask the awful taste of medicine and make precise doses possible. It was the inventions of the soft and hard capsule that would eventually lead to the decline of the pharmacist as drug-maker and the rise of the pharmacist as pill merchant.

The Burroughs Welcome company in England popularized the tablet form, beginning in the 1880s. The pills were made by a hand-operated machine that had been invented in 1843 by the English watchmaker William Brockedon. It was neither a pill-making machine nor a watch-making machine: Brockedon actually designed it to capture the waste graphite from pencil making, but it worked beautifully for packing powders into a hard form. And thus was born the tablet.

But the pharmaceutical industry didn't take over the manufacturing process for apothecaries because of economies and supe-
riority of product. The real reason was the boom in patent
medicines. Actually, "patent medicine" is a misnomer. Few of
what are called patent medicines are actually patented. The
word *patent* means "open," so the formula for any patent medicine had to be published by the patent office. No patent medicine company worth its salt (Epsom salts was the first patent
medicine in England) wanted its competitors to get hold of its
secrets. So, to protect their secrets and still get the benefits of
their product, the patent medicine companies *trademarked* their
brand names. Not that there were any great secrets to give away;
alcohol and cocaine were the main ingredients in most of these
proprietary medicines. And through massive advertising cam-
paigns, they convinced the American public to ask for their
medicines by name. Not just bitters, but Hostetters Bitters
(which was a hot-selling little patent medicine in the nineteenth
century, probably because it was 39 percent alcohol).

   In 1894, the *U.S. Pharmacopeia—the* reference book for
drugs—had no patent medicines. Ten years later, it had hundreds. These proprietary medicines had their appeals. Because
there were few doctors—and the few that there were were still
in love with bleeding and other painful cures—many people
opted for self-medication. At the turn of the century, more advertising dollars were spent to promote patent medicines than to
advertise any other product. The ads for one popular health
drink, Vin Mariani (a wine blended with Peruvian cocaine), featured testimonials from the actress Sarah Bernhardt, the inventor

Thomas Edison and President William McKinley. (It was a drink, after all, so he could safely claim he didn't inhale.)

As America headed into the twentieth century, so too did pharmacy. By 1900, every state but one had a law establishing requirements for licensing and examining pharmacists, following the lead of Rhode Island, which passed the first modern pharmacy law in 1870.

The drug companies were slowly but surely taking over the role of drugmaker. The kindly old pharmacist compounding a prescription at his table would soon give way to the kindly young pharmacist with a drug company catalog by his side. A broad knowledge of the compounding of medicines was still an essential skill for 80 percent of all prescriptions dispensed in the 1920s. By the 1940s, that had declined to 26 percent, and by 1971, it had fallen to 1 percent. Today if you see a mortar and pestle in a drugstore, it's strictly for decoration.

Chain drugstores arrived on the scene before the turn of the century. Hegeman and Company owned a string of stores in New York City; Charles Jaynes had a chain in Boston; Hall and Lyon in Providence; and a Miss Cora Dow—that's what she called herself—owned a chain of drugstores in Cincinnati. But the arrival of the chain concept to the drugstore industry can be credited to two men: Louis K. Liggett and Charles R. Walgreen. Liggett founded the United Drug Company in 1907 and within ten years operated 45 United Drugs. That's when he bought up 107 stores operated by the Riker–Hegeman–Jaynes operation, a combination of the two early chain operators. By 1930 Liggett had 672 drugstores.

Walgreen got a later start, but for those who've been indoors for a long time, his chain is now one of the dominant ones. As of this writing, there are 2,081 Walgreens drugstores. Walgreen was a clerk in a Chicago drugstore in 1905 when he got the idea to apply the economies of scale to the drugstore industry. By 1916, he owned nine Chicago drugstores, including the one where he once clerked. His chain grew exponentially: 29 stores in 1922, 116 stores by 1927 and 413 by 1947.

Chain drugstores were still minor players as the post–World War II boom began. The National Association of Chain Drugstores surveyed the situation in 1947 and found that of 52,809 drugstores in this country, only 4,655 were chains. But while chains made up only 9 percent of drugstores in number, they accounted for almost 24 percent of sales. They were a force to be reckoned with. Chains really took off after World War II, led by Liggett's latest idea: the Rexall brand.

When many people think of drugstores in the fifties—the drugstore's golden age—they think of Rexall Drugs. Every town seemed to have one. Rexall drugstores started out as "independent financial units (who) agree to purchase at least minimum amounts of Rexall products in exchange for special discounts, local and national advertising advantages and a distinctive window sign," according to the 1932 book *The Costs of Medicine.* They were like the local hardware stores associated with Ace and True Value; these drugstores bought branded products in a contract arrangement with the Rexall manufacturing company.

Liggett developed products that druggists could advise their customers to buy, over-the-counter products. Thus the name: *Rexall* stood for "Rx to all." The name became so well known that druggists asked to add it to their store names.

And thus was born the Rexall chain.

At its peak in 1950, there were 559 Rexall-owned drugstores and another 12,000 franchises. That's when new company president Justin Dart began selling off company stores. By 1955 there were only 190 company-owned stores.

Dart is an interesting story in himself. He started out as a stock boy at Walgreens, married founder Charles Walgreen's daughter Ruth, then formed Dart Industries, which bought Rexall from United Drug, in effect uniting Walgreens and Rexall.

However, his stewardship of the Rexall name was fraught with mistakes. At a time when the industry was heading toward consolidation, he was selling off company stores. In 1969 Dart sold Rexall's prescription-drug manufacturing facilities. By the time he sold Rexall in 1977, the sale price was a mere $16 million—a fraction of what it was once worth. That's how far Rexall had fallen.

In 1980, under new president Larry Weber, Rexall shifted its emphasis to distribution. Weber pared the list of Rexall products from 650 to 470. The company's biggest sellers were plastic toothbrushes and hairbrushes. Weber added 124 health-related products to the line: vitamins, herbal teas, dried fruits. That didn't work either.

Today Rexall is part of Rexall Sundown, having been purchased by a small south Florida sunburn-cream firm.

The once-giant Rexall name is now splattered across the landscape in a hit-or-miss pattern. There are 427 drugstores still operating under the Rexall banner, but they have nothing to do with the formerly mighty Rexall chain. In the eighties, after Rexall got out of the retail business, it allowed some stores to keep the Rexall name.

The names today, in addition to Walgreens, are Rite-Aid and Revco. Combined the chains own 28,381 drugstores, about 52 percent of the nation's drugstores, and do 84 percent of the drugstore business.

The trend is unmistakable; we are heading toward bigger drugstores owned by national companies. One hundred years ago, in 1897, there were 39,885 drugstores serving a population of only 70 million, or about one store per 1,750 people. Today there are 54,515 drugstores serving a population of 260 million, or one store per 4,770 people. Independent drugstores no longer outnumber chain stores. Corner drugstores are going out of business at the rate of four a day, according to *The Economist*. At that rate, the chain drugstores will walk on the old corner drug's tombstone sometime in the next twenty years. That may be an historic event, but not one I am looking forward to.

What happened to the old corner drug? The same thing that happened to the old corner hardware and corner grocery. Changing times and changing retail climates.

The fifties were the golden age for many retail businesses. Chains and franchises were just starting to arrive on the retail front. The little guy really could take out a second mortgage and start a business that would make him self-employed and self-fulfilled.

Price was important to shoppers then. Price has always been an important part of the retail mix. But service was equally important. Then came something called self-service. It revolutionized the grocery store, turning the survivors into supermarkets. This self-service trend hit other industries, too. Hardware stores no longer kept everything behind the counter. Customers were encouraged to find their way through the store, find it themselves and bring it to a central cash register location.

The same thing happened in the drugstore. Old Doc Friendly

had been adding items to his stock all along: film and batteries to go along with film processing, greeting cards to send the sick and the grieving. It wouldn't all fit behind the counter. That's when drugstores joined the self-service age. To mind the store— pharmacists still spent much of their time filling prescriptions— Doc elevated his pharmacy department. He put it up on a platform so he could look out over the entire store. That tradition continues at many drugstores, although security cameras and security guards make it unnecessary.

As drugstores became more than just pharmacies, they began to compete with other specialty stores. Groceries sold candy; pharmacies sold candy. Soon groceries were carrying health and beauty aids, and drugstores were carrying potato chips and packaged confections.

The modern super drugstore is a natural progression that began in pharmacies back in Fibber McGee's day. The corner drug couldn't stay just a corner drug—because it was no longer just the corner drug. It had become what McGee's announcer said it was: part department store, part hospital, part book nook and candy kitchen, part post office and short-order restaurant. The leeches were now the out-of-state corporations that bought out old Doc Friendly and demanded increased sales and higher returns from their corporate managers. The drugstore manager was no longer a pharmacist.

Drugstores—at least many of them—are no longer community centers. They are shopping centers.

We wanted lower prices and larger selections at the corner drug and we got them. And the price we've paid is that the corner drug sold out to National Corner Drug, Inc. If it's not a profit center, it's gone. So good-bye soda fountain, good-bye cosmetics counter, good-bye good old Doc Friendly. Say hello to low prices, large selection and . . . what was your name again, Mr. Pharmacist?

FAMOUS PHARMACISTS

Antiquity had no famous pharmacists. It barely had any famous people—a few guys whose last names were The Conqueror, a couple called The Elder and a The Terrible or two.

The first famous pharmacist in history was Louis Hebert, who abandoned his French *apothicaire* in 1608 to accompany Champlain on his exploration of the New World. There weren't a whole lot of pharmacists clamoring to settle the New World. The only other early settler–pharmacist was John Johnstone, of Edinburgh, who led the group that founded Perth Amboy, New Jersey, in 1638.

There was a serious scarcity of pharmacists in the colonies, and in 1621 the Virginia colony offered to pay the children's transportation if an apothecary and his wife would settle anywhere in Virginia. There were no takers.

The first pharmacist–congressman was Ray Vaughn Pierce, elected from the Buffalo, New York, district in 1878. Pierce was the creator of the Golden Medical Discovery, a popular patent medicine of the time.

The first pharmacist–scientist was Swedish pharmacist Karl Wilhelm Scheele, who discovered oxygen in 1773. No, people weren't holding their breath until someone discovered it. Scheele isn't usually given credit for the discovery because the Brit Joseph Priestly performed a similar experiment and published first. Scheele also discovered chlorine, arsenic, citric acid and lactic acid. And we thank him for those discoveries.

Atlanta pharmacist John S. Pemberton mixed seltzer water with sugar and cocaine—okay, okay, with coca leaves—to invent Coca-Cola. And we thank him for it.

And New Orleans pharmacist Antoine Peychard got the idea to mix tonics of cognac with his own bitters and serve it in an eggcup (the French word for eggcup is *coquetier*), thereby creating what we now know as the cocktail. And we really thank him for it.

Infamous might be a better term for Dr. John Brinkley, a former meat cutter who introduced pharmacy to radio advertising. Brinkley, who had purchased his medical diploma for $100 in St. Louis, bought a closed drugstore in Milford, Kansas, and took to the airwaves with his famous cure for "failing manhood" (no explanation for what "failing manhood" meant was necessary then . . . or now). He transplanted goat glands into human, uh, glands with results that were, according to his radio broadcasts, remarkable. He was wildly successful, building his own radio station, KFKB in Milford, buying his wife Buick-sized diamonds and touring the country in his private plane. Brinkley signed up 1,500 members for his Brinkley Pharmaceutical Association, franchise pharmacists who sold his concoctions by number. Numbers 2, 16 and 17 were for mothers. He told nursing mothers in his radio audience, "If her druggist hasn't got them, she should write and order them from the Milford Drug Company, Milford, Kansas, and they will be sent to you, Mother, collect. May the Lord guard and protect you, Mother. The postage will be prepaid." In 1930 the government caught up with Dr. Brinkley and forced him across the border to Mexico, where he built a 100,000-watt station, XER, and continued to hawk his goat-gland cures for another ten years, until shut down by a U.S.–Mexican treaty, the only pharmacist ever to become the subject of international diplomacy.

The first famous American-born pharmacist would become famous in another field. His name as a pharmacist was William Sydney Porter, but when he changed professions he also changed names, becoming . . . O. Henry. You know the rest of the story.

Or maybe not. He traded his medicine bottles for the basic tool of the writing trade: the gin bottle. O. Henry died at age forty-seven, a penniless alcoholic. Like most of the writers I know.

There have been a number of famous fictional pharmacists.

Doc Hackett, proprietor of Hackett Drugs, was the star of *County Seat,* a radio drama that ran for one season, 1938–39, on CBS. Hackett, played by Ray Collins, was the druggist in the small town of Northbury. The show was created by a real pharmacist, Milton Geiger, who went on to write many radio and TV dramas, as well as the Broadway play *Edwin Booth.*

Ed Kremer, proprietor of Kremer's Drugstore in Wistful Vista, was the most famous fictional pharmacist of the first half of the twentieth century. Kremer filled prescriptions and dispensed good advice and bad jokes to Fibber McGee and Molly on the long-running radio comedy of the same name. *Fibber McGee* was one of the most popular radio shows of its time (1934–52), making Kremer one of the most famous pharmacists of all time. Kremer's was a corner drug, located at the intersection of fourteenth and Oak, an inside joke among the show's writers, who would give every store in Wistful Vista that address.

Kremer was played by a half-dozen actors during the show's long run, including Ed Begley, Sr.; John McIntyre; Howard McNear (later famous as Floyd the barber on *The Andy Griffith Show*) and even William Conrad, who later gave voice to Matt Dillon on radio's *Gunsmoke.*

A typical exchange between Kremer and the McGees would go like this:

KREMER: Here you are, McGee. I hope this fixes up that sprained ankle all right.
MOLLY: Sprained ankle? The prescription was for a gargle, Mr. Kremer.
KREMER: That's all right. It won't hurt his ankle either.
McGEE: But I ain't got a sprained ankle.
KREMER: Look, McGee. I had five other druggists look at the prescription at a Rotary luncheon this noon. And all but one of us agreed it was for a sprained ankle. The other thought it was a Chinese laundry ticket. Who are you to argue with five druggists? That'll be a dollar-eighty.

When *The Great Gildersleeve* show was spun off *Fibber,* the new show acquired its own druggist. Richard Q. Peavey of Peavey's Pharmacy was the family pharmacist for the Gildersleeves. Mr. Peavey, played from 1941 to 1958 by Richard LeGrand, was a sitcom unto himself as he bantered with Throckmorton Gildersleeve. During a brief fling with opera, Gildy convinced Peavey to help him sell opera tickets. When he discovered the druggist hadn't sold a one, Gildersleeve was offended. Peavey offered as how people didn't normally ask for opera tickets at his drugstore: "People come in and ask for a lot of things. I had a woman come in and ask for a dozen and a half skate keys once. . . . It was just by the merest chance that I happened to have them." In 1950 the National Association of Retail Druggists named Peavey "America's Favorite Neighborhood Druggist."

The most famous film pharmacist is probably Mr. Gower (H. B. Warner), the alcoholic druggist in *It's a Wonderful Life,* who in a drunken state put poison in a prescription. It would have cost a kid his life had not young Jimmy Stewart refused to deliver the bottle. Jimmy got his due, but not before Mr. Gower boxed his ears for insubordination.

The only film starring a pharmacist was the 1942 Western *In Old California,* with John Wayne—John Wayne!—as a druggist struggling to make a go of it in the gold rush days. (When pharmacists watch this movie, they are inevitably distracted by the Duke's anachronistic medicine bottles, which have indentations for labels some ten years before such bottles were created. The lesson, of course, is don't watch this movie with a pharmacist.)

Television's most famous pharmacist was Miss Ellie (Elinor Donahue), Andy Griffith's sometime sweetie on *The Andy Griffith Show.* When Miss Ellie finally saw the light that Andy was a confirmed bachelor and took up with a young doctor, her epitaph from the show was spoken by Barney Fife, who shook his head and muttered, "Two young people, lost in a world of pills."

Famous Pharmacies

There are two famous drugstores in America, and most people have never been to either one of them.

Schwab's, on Sunset Boulevard, was the place of Hollywood legend—where Lana Turner was discovered, where Ava Gardner bought her lipstick, where Marilyn Monroe left messages for gossip columnist Sidney Skolsky and where everyone who was anyone stopped and shopped. Wall Drug, in Wall, South Dakota, is the place of tourist legend.

If you haven't been to Schwab's, you can't go now. It was torn down in 1988. A Virgin Records store stands on the site. You can go to Wall. It's just that it's way the hell away from anywhere.

Schwab's was the original place to see and be seen. Its reputation was solidified—not that it needed to be—in the 1950 film *Sunset Blvd.,* when hack screenwriter Joe Gillis told the audience, "I drove down to headquarters. That's the way a lot of us think about Schwab's. Kind of a combination office, kaffeeklatsch and waiting room. Waiting, waiting for the gravy train."

Schwab's arrived in Hollywood shortly after Jack Warner and Sam Goldwyn and all the studio moguls. In 1932, pharmacist Jack Schwab moved his little downtown drugstore to the corner of Sunset Boulevard and Crescent Heights, in the heart of the Sunset Strip. It was a bustling area: across the street was the Garden of Allah Hotel, where F. Scott Fitzgerald and Robert Benchley gathered each afternoon to drown their Hollywood sorrows. Ciro's and the Mocambo were down the street. There was action in every direction: bookies and newsboys, barbers and shoe-shine boys.

Schwab's first attracted the Hollywood elite because it was the only place open at 7 A.M. Early risers made it a breakfast favorite. It didn't hurt that doctor-to-the-stars Dr. Frank Nolan had his office next door.

The one event that made Schwab's the Hollywood hangout was *Photoplay* magazine's gossip columnist Sidney Skolsky taking an apartment two doors down in 1933. It was he who created the legend by writing about all of the drugstore's celebrity

customers. Skolsky spent so much time there that Jack Schwab
even gave him a drawer at the prescription counter where he
could store his notes.

Marion Davies, Errol Flynn, Rita Hayworth and Marilyn
Monroe all had their prescriptions filled at Schwab's. The store's
delivery boy dropped a single sleeping pill off at Judy Garland's
house each evening.

But it was the soda fountain that made Schwab's a legend.
Soda fountain regulars included Charlie Chaplin, Orson Welles,
Howard Duff and Ava Gardner, and in later years Jack Nicholson, Western novelist Louis L'Amour and James Dean. The
soda fountain drew droves of small-town beauty queens over the
years, each hoping to follow in the footsteps—or C-cups—of
Lana Turner, who was supposedly discovered there by a Hollywood producer attracted by her porcelain skin, high cheekbones
and two-sizes-too-small argyle sweater. The beauty queens with
their desperate dreams of stardom would be immortalized in
Sunset Blvd. as "cantaloupe queens and dinner whores."

The enduring legend of Lana Turner, is, alas, false. She
wasn't discovered at Schwab's. But she was discovered at a
soda fountain: the Top Hat Soda Shop, a soda fountain and café
located about a mile away, across the street from Hollywood
High. Seventeen-year-old Turner, then known as Judy Turner,
was sitting at the Top Hat's fountain sipping a Coke when Billy
Wilkerson, the publisher of the *Hollywood Reporter,* hit on her:
"Every pretty young girl wants to be in the movies, and I think
you'd be perfect."

She was.

Wall Drug has a different kind of fame, the kind born of dili-
gent self-promotion and sustained by quality service. It is the

Burma-Shave of this era. Its virtues are expounded on billboards all over the West.

FRESH CINNAMON ROLLS
WALL DRUG

SEE WESTERN ORIGINAL
OIL PAINTINGS
AT WALL DRUG

Their road signs don't exactly have the panache of the old Burma-Shave quatrains.

"Free ice water at Wall Drug" hardly compares to "Henry the 8th/Sure Had Trouble/Short Term Wives/Long Term Stubble," but road-weary tourists heading out of the Black Hills will take ice water over iambic pentameter any day.

Wall Drug has been a beacon for tourists since 1931, when young pharmacist Ted Hustead and his wife, Dorothy, took over the operation of the local pharmacy. It was not an auspicious time to go into business; most of the locals were either unemployed or working for warrants from a bankrupt local government. But the Husteads stuck it out. And that western determination, combined with free ice water, helped them hang on through the Dust Bowl and Depression days.

Today Wall Drug is as famous in the West as Rock City once was in the South. The store covers more than an acre, a healthy chunk of downtown Wall. There are four dining rooms serving as many as 5,000 meals a day. Tourists can buy souvenirs, jewelry, camping gear, postcards, western wear, books.

And, oh yeah, drugs.

3
From Head to Toe:
Starting, Naturally Enough, with the Head

The major mission of the drugstore is your good health. If drugstores have a boast, it's that they can take care of you from head to toe.

From that unruly mop on top to that bunion on your big toe, drugstores are there for you. And so is this book. That's why I've organized the chapters from head to toe. The drugstore items that you use for your head, from hair tonic to headache remedies, are covered in this chapter. And if you are wondering about that bunion medicine, turn to the Foot and Leg chapter near the end of the book.

Bayer Aspirin—100-Count Bottle—$3.29

It's giving me a headache just comparing all the different brands of pain relievers. By my count there are twenty-six different brands—that's brands!—in the health and beauty aids aisle of the Drug Emporium. That doesn't account for all the varieties within brands: Tylenol Regular, Extra Strength Tylenol, Tylenol

Regular Gelcap, and on and on and on. There are ten different varieties of Tylenol alone.

Tylenol, in all its various forms, is the number-one best-selling product in the drugstore. Not just this section—the entire drugstore. In 1995, the last year for which I could find statistics, Americans bought $329 million worth of Tylenol. That was a healthy $75 million more than the number-two drugstore product, Revlon cosmetics.

So how did we get from a bottle of aspirin to bottles and bottles of Bayer and Bufferin, Advil and Anacin, Extra Strength Tylenol and Excedrin? One pill at a time.

In the beginning was willow bark. Yes, the bark of a common willow tree. It's doubtful that Hippocrates was the first to pulverize the bark, turning it into a powder that he used to treat patients with pains. He undoubtedly used an older recipe, probably one from the Egyptians. But in the fifth century B.C. he manufactured this bitter powder and gave it to his patients to relieve pain. It was the original bitter pill.

And while he probably didn't discover the drug, he is the first to get credit for using this early form of aspirin, because he had the good sense to write down everything he did. (Wasn't it Winston Churchill who said, "History will treat me kindly because I intend to write that history"? Same thing.)

The formula for this miracle—for 400 B.C.—drug was somehow lost for a couple of millennia, then rediscovered in 1758 by the English clergy, who also figured out that willow bark relieved pain. This was the Age of Science, so scientists set out to determine why willow bark worked this way. By 1820 they had isolated the key ingredient, salicin, a pharmacological cousin of the salicylates. This stuff was great—it relieved pain—but it also *was* a pain, a pain in the stomach. (Today, unbuffered aspirin still gives many people an upset stomach.)

It took a French chemist, Charles Frederic Gerhardt, to solve the stomach problem. In 1853, he combined sodium salicylate with acetyl chloride—and voilà, or eureka might be a better term—no headache, no stomachache.

Gerhardt published his experiments, but apparently no one was reading. He saw no future for his little chemical compound and moved on. It would be almost half a century before someone picked up on his miracle drug.

In 1897, Felix Hoffmann, a chemist for the German firm Friederich Bayer & Company—see where this is heading?—was searching for a drug to help relieve his arthritic father's pain without irritating his stomach. He read Gerhardt's paper, duplicated the compound, and soon his father was dancing the polka.

Hoffmann convinced Bayer to manufacture the miracle drug. They named it "aspirin," combining the A of acetyl chloride with the SPIR of *Spiraea ulmaria,* the plant that produced salicylic acid. The result was ASPIR, which looked too much like the name for a breathing medication. So they added the IN, a common suffix for medicines at the time.

And aspirin was born.

The first Bayer aspirin was a powder. It wasn't until 1915 that Bayer introduced tablets. The company actually trademarked the tablet design, with the familiar A on the pill (the company also trademarked an H tablet for heroin, but that's another story). However, the company lost the trademark in the Treaty of Versailles in 1919. Honest. As part of war reparations, the A tablet trademark was turned over to the Allies. They didn't want the Germans benefiting from anything, receiving any payments from the West—even something as insignificant as an aspirin trademark royalty.

Soon everyone was turning out aspirin. And TV was overrun by commercials of little *A*s racing little *B*s to your pain. Aspirin was king in the fifties. When people got a headache, they had two choices. They could take an aspirin. Or they could take two aspirin. But scientists, being the crafty guys they are, soon developed other pain relievers. And little *A*s had to race little *B*s and little *T*s and all manner of pain relievers.

Today, despite the fact that there are scores of products on the drugstore shelves, there are really only five different pain relievers. The commercials want you to think there are more, but analgesics as a whole can be divided into five parts: aspirin, acetaminophen, ibuprofen, naproxen sodium and ketoprofen.

Aspirin you know about. That's what this whole section has been on. Variations include Anacin, which combines aspirin and caffeine, and Bufferin, which "buffers" the aspirin with an antacid that helps prevent stomach irritation.

The second category—and present favorite—is acetaminophen. Tylenol is acetaminophen, as are Panadol and some one hundred other pain relievers. Excedrin is a blend of acetaminophen, aspirin and caffeine.

The most famous member of the third category, the ibuprofen family, is Advil. Others include Motrin, Nuprin, Midol (for menstrual cramps) and fifty or so others.

Midol is nothing fancy. It's just ibuprofen with 32 mg of caffeine. That's right, the only difference between Advil and Midol is the caffeine. You don't feel the pain and you're excited about it.

Aleve has the naproxen sodium group all to itself. That's because Aleve's parent company still owns exclusive rights in the over-the-counter market.

The last of the five pain relievers is ketoprofen, which only received FDA approval for over-the-counter sales in 1995. Names to note here are Orudis KT and Actron.

Aspirin is now in second place in the pain relief section, behind acetaminophen (Tylenol et al.). But it's still a profitable place to be; you and I would certainly settle for second in this market. Even in second place, aspirin sold $700 million worth of pills in 1996. But that was dwarfed by the $1.4 billion that Tylenol and its cousins racked up. The other painkillers combined had another $700 million in sales. The Tylenol family accounts for half of all the pain relievers sold.

Bayer is the best-selling aspirin and fifth overall among pain relievers. That's still good for about $100 million in annual sales. Aspirin sales may be declining, but Americans still take some 80 billion aspirin tablets a year.

It works for them.

How? A couple of millennia after Hippocrates, we still don't know exactly. Ask a scientist and you'll hear something about inhibiting prostaglandin production. Since that's probably the first time you've ever heard the word prostaglandin, that probably doesn't mean much to you. It's a hormone thing, you wouldn't understand. I don't.

If you talk to drugstore people about aspirin and Tylenol and all the other pain relievers, eventually you will hear one of them refer to it as the analgesic market. That's the industry term. *Analgesic* comes from the Latin, *anal* for butt and *gesic* for hurts. No, that's not right. It comes from the Greek *analgesia,* which means "want of feeling." That's *want* as in *don't want—*

don't want to feel the pain. Druggists lump all pain relievers to-gether—and lump them all into one section, the section that gives me a headache just looking at it. This one.

Bufferin Arthritis Strength—100-Count Bottle with Childproof Cap—$9.89

My mother is a senior citizen (okay, she doesn't want me pub-lishing her age) and the only thing she doesn't like is taking her medicine. She doesn't mind the diabetes pill or the blood pres-sure pill. She minds the bottle. She has a dickens of a time opening those childproof caps. Childproof, yes, but also senior citizen proof.

Thanks, Abe Plough. Abe's the man who invented the child-proof cap, the scourge of modern times. And he didn't *have* to in-vent it. He did it because he was sure it was the right thing to do.

Okay, let's give Abe some credit. Actually, lots of credit. When he was head of Plough Laboratories, he put his research team to work on a medicine bottle cap that would be difficult to open. It was during the fifties and at the suggestion of Dr. Jay Arena, then head of Duke University's Poison Control Center. Arena was concerned that children were opening up pill bot-tles—hey, they're kids, they're supposed to be curious—swal-lowing the contents and dying. He asked Plough if his company couldn't come up with a cap that would be, in Arena's words, "hard to get into."

Plough's team did and Plough started using it on his number-one product, St. Joseph's Aspirin for Children. This was in 1957, long before the Child Resistant Product Act of 1970, long before product liability, long before lawyers advertised for product liability clients.

And it has worked remarkably over the years. A 1992 study in the *Journal of the American Medical Association* showed that childhood fatalities from accidental pill swallowing—"unintentional ingestion of oral prescription drugs"—dropped from 3.5 per million to 2.0 per million in the quarter century after hard-to-get-into caps were mandated for all drugs. Admittedly, safety consciousness—some might say obsessiveness—has also increased among moms during that time period. But who's to say the childproof hard-to-get-into cap didn't also contribute to that consciousness.

The childproof cap wasn't Plough's only contribution to children's medicine. He also made St. Joseph's the most child-friendly aspirin on the market. Its tablets were child-size, one-fourth the size of regular aspirin. They were also chewable—no more "Gulp hard, dear"—and orange flavored, to make them more palatable to small palates.

The latter may have been the most important contribution, at least from a former kid's point of view. Before St. Joseph's, just the thought of that aspirin taste and I thought I was going to die.

The discovery that Reye's syndrome was caused by aspirin has all but killed St. Joseph's Aspirin for Children and all children's aspirin, but not before St. Joseph and its benefactor gave the world the childproof cap. The children of the world thank them. Those of us who hate opening childproof caps are on the fence on this one.

And anyone who has arthritis bad enough to need Bufferin Arthritis Strength will probably also need someone to open the childproof cap for them.

Sominex Original Formula—32 Tablets—$5.19

When I was in college, I went through a period of insomnia. I don't know what caused it: academic-induced stress, dormitory-induced stress, girlfriend-induced stress. Whatever, I would lie in bed, staring at the clock, calculating how much sleep I would get if I fell asleep immediately. Doing math didn't help my condition. Finally, after a month or so of wandering into class late in a sleep-deprived stupor, I gave in. I bought Sominex. It didn't help me go to sleep any quicker. I would still lie there doing math on the clock. But when I eventually did fall asleep, I slept like a log, right through the alarm, right through the first class, right through the midterm, and almost right out the door. I quickly gave up Sominex and went back to my regular old insomnia. And in another few weeks, it too passed.

Insomnia and college students are a matched pair. A recent study of Penn State students' sleeping habits showed that 78.8 percent of women and 71.3 percent of males had trouble falling asleep at least one night a month. Of those who reported sleep problems, 6.4 percent of males and 11.4 percent of females admitted using over-the-counter sleep aids, such as Sominex or Compoz or Nytol.

So what is it about Sominex that puts you to sleep? An antihistamine. Sominex is an antihistamine. So not only does it induce sleep, it clears up your sinuses. You know, I sort of recall not having any cold symptoms while I was on Sominex.

Sominex is for when you want to sleep but don't want to use illegal drugs.

It has been the punchline for a thousand jokes and chides. It is a regular feature of movie reviews in this country. Usually

the reviewer will point out that a given film or show will help
an audience get to sleep far better than Sominex could.

Q-Tips—Package of 100—$1.29

If Leo Gerstenzang hadn't invented Q-Tips, someone else surely
would have. It's just too wonderful a product not to exist.

Gerstenzang, a Polish-born, naturalized American citizen,
was watching his wife give their baby daughter a bath one day
in 1923. He was taken with the way she cleaned out the baby's
ears: twirling a ball of cotton on the end of a toothpick and using this as a swab. What a wonderful thing, he marveled. Since
he already owned Leo Gerstenzang Infant Novelty Co., it was
just a short trip from observation to manufacture of a ready-
made cotton swab. According to "The Fascinating Story of Q-
Tips Brand Products," a manufacturer's pamphlet, he called his
new product Baby Gays. At this late date we don't know why.
We do know that at my house we've been calling them Baby
Gays ever since I uncovered this startling fact, as sort of an exercise in what-if. What if he hadn't renamed the swab Q-Tips
from Baby Gays in 1926? Think how the history of this country
might be different.

But he did and it isn't. Q-Tip was a bastardization of *cotton-
tip,* very much a bastardization.

Today Q-tips are used for more than just cleaning out baby's
ears. In fact, I'll be cleaning my tape recorder heads here in just
a minute. Could you hand me one of those Baby Gays?

4
The Hair:
Or Sometimes Lack Thereof

Bald may be beautiful in the NBA, but for most of history and for most of the world, bald has been a bummer.

Ovid, the Roman Rod McKuen, wrote in A.D. 10:

Ugly is a field without grass,
A plant without leaves,
Or a head without hair.

Thanks, Ovid.

This negativity about baldness started with Samson, the biblical superman. Judges 16:17 records: "If I be shaved, then my strength will leave me, and I shall become weak and be like any other man." You know the story: Samson woos Delilah, she sells him out to the Philistines, he takes a nap and wakes up bald and sapped of his mighty strength. They gouge out his eyes and turn him into a slave. But the hair grows back and he brings down the house, killing a cast of thousands. And the movie ends. But bald already has a bad name.

The first hair-growing elixir (satisfaction guaranteed or your drachmas back) was created in 4000 B.C. by the mother of

Egypt's King Chata. Her formula: grind up dates, dogs' paws and asses' hooves, cook in oil, rub vigorously into scalp. Archaeologists have never found her son's tomb, so we don't know how well the potion worked.

Our old friend Hippocrates, who worried about his bald spot, became the first man of medicine to concoct a cure for baldness. He mixed horseradish, beetroot, spices, opium and pigeon droppings. Then he noticed that eunuchs didn't have a problem with baldness. He tossed his horseradish–beetroot–spice–opium–pigeon droppings potion and chose baldness over eunuch-ness.

The first recorded instance of male pattern baldness vanity can be traced to Hannibal—"The Carthage Conqueror"—who had a wig made to cover his receding hairline. He liked it so much he wore it into battle. He won, and soon aspiring conquerors all over were sporting toupees.

Julius Caesar, unhappy with an inability to divide and conquer his growing baldness, invented the comb-over, combing hair from the rear of his head forward to cover his bald spot. Still unable to conquer the baldness, he invented the Dennis Rodman look, wearing a laurel wreath that gave him the appearance of having green hair. He went so far as to arm-twist the Roman senate into passing a law that allowed him to wear his laurel wreath twenty-four hours a day.

The final straw for bald men may have come in A.D. 100, when the church declared that the wearing of a wig made from someone else's hair was a mortal sin. The search was on for a cure for baldness.

Galen, the Roman physician often called the father of anatomy, founded an early version of the Hair Club for Men in A.D. 122, advising his patients they could prevent baldness by avoiding mushrooms and toadstools.

Bald Is Beautiful had a brief renaissance in 1521, when France's King Francis I led his minions in a bit of high jinks, a snowball attack on next-door neighbor Count Montgomery. The count's men dropped a torch on the snowballers, burning Francis's hair off. The burns were so severe that the king was thereafter bald. His courtiers followed his lead, shaving their own heads to emulate the king.

But this affinity for baldness was short-lived. When Louis XIII went bald at age twenty-four, he adopted the piled-high white wig as his signature look. Soon, all of seventeenth-century France was overtaken by Big Hair.

Samuel Pepys wrote the first self-help manual for baldies. In his diary he recorded his first venture into public with his wig: "I found that coming [to church] in a periwig did not prove so strange as I was afraid it would for I thought that all the church would presently have cast their eyes upon me, but I found no such things."

Time marches forward to America the (Bald and) Beautiful! Six of the first eight presidents were bald or balding and unashamed: George Washington, John Adams, James Madison, James Monroe, John Quincy Adams and Martin Van Buren.

Then, in A.D. 1804, Napoleon set bald men back a thousand years with the return of the comb-over. He pulled all he could find in the rear forward, a strategy he later adopted, to disastrous results, at Waterloo.

Balding Dr. John Breck, desperately searching for a way to hold on to his hair, invented modern shampoo in 1908. His concoction, Breck Shampoo, became a big hit, even though it didn't keep Breck from becoming bald.

Bald Is Beautiful, Part 2: In 1953, Yul Brynner landed the

lead in the Broadway musical *The King and I* and became the first bald sex symbol.

Two decades later, Telly Savalas became television's first bald leading man with the debut of the detective series *Kojak*.

The Bald Is Beautiful campaign received another setback in the nineties when Ron Popeil, founder of K-Tel and creator of hundreds of gimcrack inventions (the Smokeless Ashtray, the Pocket Fisherman, the Vegematic), introduced his crowning— pun intended—achievement, GLH Formula #9, a hair thickener that helped insecure bald men hide that see-through spot by painting their heads. GLH stood for Good Looking Hair.

As we stand on the threshold of a new millennium, we have conclusive proof that not only can bald be beautiful, it can also be sexy. Witness Sean Connery, Bruce Willis, Ed Harris, Jack Nicholson, Willard Scott. (Well, maybe not Willard Scott.) But despite this self-evident truth, most bald men would prefer not to be bald. How else to explain the fact that Upjohn's stock jumped in the early eighties just on the rumor that its nerve medicine minoxidil *might* grow hair. And when the Food and Drug Administration approved Rogaine, the trade name for mi- noxidil—the first hair-growing ointment ever approved by the FDA—in 1988, Upjohn stock zoomed.

Rogaine—8-Ounce Bottle—$29.95

Rogaine was a slam dunk. Anyone could have predicted the rush it would cause. That's because half of all men begin losing sig- nificant amounts of hair before age forty. By age eighty, most men are bald.

It is genes, not bad diet or too much sex (I started that old wives' tale myself), that determines your hair's fate. My mother insisted for years that my baldness came from my father's side. My father argued the opposite. The fact is that the bald gene can be inherited from either side.

Baldness is caused by dihydrotestosterone (DHT), a form of testosterone, attacking the hair follicle and causes it to shrink. Scientists say that at one time I had about 100,000 hairs on my head. (If I had been a blond, that number would be 120,000, because blond hair is thinner; if I had been a redhead, it would have been only 80,000, because red hair is thicker.) I now have about 50,000 hairs. No, I didn't count. I'll take science's word for it.

Some 35 million men in this country are losing or have lost their hair to male pattern baldness, according to the American Hair Loss Council, a trade group that I'll bet doesn't show up on political campaign contribution lists.

I am one of those 35 million men.

I'm no different from other bald men. I love not buying hair tonic, I love not carrying a comb and I love not living in the fear of the wind. But, given the choice, I would choose hair. That's why I am at the Rogaine display, money in hand, pride in pocket.

I've been bald for twenty years. I remember how it started. First came denial.

I was twenty-one and combing my hair in my dorm room when Bevo Francis, who lived across the hall, peeked in and said, "You're losing your hair."

"No, I'm not," I replied, perhaps a bit too quickly. "I just have a high forehead."

I am not losing my hair. I am not losing my hair. Repeat after me: I am not losing my hair.

Then I started noticing that the bathtub drain was always clogging up with hair. So I started spending more time in front

of the mirror staring at my high forehead. I would lift up the
front lock and gaze intently. It's always been that way, I assured
myself. I've always had a high forehead.

I've always had a high forehead.

I've always had a high forehead.

Next came step two: recognition. During one of my marathon
stare-at-my-hairline sessions, I noticed that where my front lock
swept backward I could see bottom.

It's going. Oh God, it's going. I'm only twenty-two years old
and my hair is going.

Recognition quickly gave way to a third stage: cover-up. I began to part my hair lower on the side and bring more of it forward to cover the thin spots. By the time I was twenty-four, I
was afraid even to lift up the front lock. I knew what was under
there: Nothing!

I was desperate—desperate enough to try anything. I mas-
saged my forehead. My mother rubbed Vaseline into my thin-
ning pate because she had heard that it would cure baldness. I
even ordered a cream that was supposed to aid hair growth. The
massage made my fingers sore. The Vaseline made my head
shiny—just what a bald man wants! And the cream smelled
worse than acne ointment.

So at age twenty-five I entered the fourth—and what I
thought was the final—stage: resignation. I was bald. I would be
forever bald. I must accept that I was a bald man. I was getting
tired of living in fear of the wind.

So I accepted it. What did it matter? What's a little hair on the
head? Was I less attractive to the opposite sex? Two of the
biggest sex symbols in America at the time were bald: Yul Brynner and Telly Savalas. And think of all the money I would save
on hair goo. Lots of people are bald and live with it.

I convinced myself that I was not vain. I believed it. I may still. May.

Then, about ten years ago, I started hearing about this experimental blood-pressure medicine, minoxidil, that had achieved remarkable results in growing hair on bald men. I even got a letter inviting me to participate in one of the test studies. I pondered it. (I was more curious about how they knew to send me a letter—can you buy a mailing list of bald men?) But the words *guinea pig* kept appearing in my thoughts. So I turned the offer down.

Minoxidil was eventually approved as a hair-growing drug—with many caveats: it takes time, hair regrowth varies with individuals, it may not work. It was given the trade name Rogaine and introduced to the market in 1988, to much fanfare.

Manufacturer Upjohn's stock climbed based simply on the fact that this new wonder drug "might" grow hair. After all, a hair-growing medicine has long been touted as the better mousetrap of the drug industry.

When Rogaine hit the market, I thought some more about it. I read all the stories and studied the fine print. But the fine print that said fifty dollars a month and no guarantees convinced me to pass again. After all, I'm bald and I'm used to it. This is me. And besides, many of my friends have caught up with me. For them hair loss is an age thing. Hah! Not me.

Then I saw on TV that Rogaine had gone over-the-counter. No doctor visits. Just run down to the friendly neighborhood apothecary, plop down the money and—in the privacy of my own home—grow hair.

So I decided I should try to grow hair. I can't even grow tomatoes and I'm going to grow hair?

But if it does come back, what will it look like? Will it be gray, like much of what's left? Or will it be red, like my beard?

And will it be poker-straight, the way it was back in the six-ties? Or will I be a curly-headed fool?

I am not a prime candidate for Rogaine. I have more hair loss than the box recommends. And while I do fit into the demo-graphic group that had the best results—white men between eighteen and forty-nine—I have had hair loss for longer than is optimal.

My pharmacist doesn't discount the possibility that my hair will grow back. "If the hair follicles are just constricted, it'll work. If they're dead, they're dead."

He also loaned me a tape that Rogaine sends to pharmacists so they can better advise potential customers. The tape says hair loss can negatively effect men in five areas:

1. Masculinity
2. Appearance
3. Attractiveness
4. Youth
5. Health

Let's examine those five points.

Am I less masculine because of hair loss? I don't think so, and I've never thought so. If anything, I thought the other way. Bald is more masculine. The meanest professional wrestlers were always the bald ones. And when I was a kid, the rumor was that baldness was caused by too much testosterone, the hor-mone that makes professional boxers and NFL linemen love to hit each other.

Does it effect my appearance? Of course it does. I don't have any hair on top. In and of itself that doesn't matter.

Which brings us to number three: attractiveness. This is the hot button for bald men. We do think that. We do believe it makes us less attractive.

Number four: youth. Yes, it makes you look older. Believe me, in my twenties, this was not a problem. I never got carded at nightclubs, while all my friends had to dig in their pants and purses to find their IDs. You are going to have to accept the aging process at some point (unless you are Warren Beatty). Here hair loss helps.

And finally, health. Yes, exposure to the sun can cause skin cancer and baldness exposes more skin. So wear a hat. That'll protect your forehead, too, something Rogaine can't help.

I believe the obsession with baldness is a vanity thing. If we American men could get over that, Upjohn stock would plummet.

But we can't.

And so I stand here, Rogaine in hand. I worry that it won't work, condemning me to be bald for the rest of my life because there is no hair-growing miracle drug on the horizon.

But even more I think I worry that it might work. A lifetime of denial and recognition and resignation for naught. What would I do with hair?

I'll check back in on the Rogaine experiment later in the book.

Vitalis with V7—4-Ounce Bottle—$4.99

This may be the smallest section in the drugstore: hair tonic. There are two brands, Vitalis and Brylcreem. In my father's day—when men wore hats (not ball caps) and women wore gloves—hair tonic was an important part of every man's toiletry kit. There was the razor, the shaving cream, the shaving cup, the shaving brush, the Old Spice aftershave and the hair tonic. And for my father, and probably your father, that hair tonic was Vitalis. With V7!

The hair tonic market died a slow death in the early seventies, when hippies made the wild, unkempt look a style. The commercial that spelled the end was the one that went: "The wet head is dead. Long live the dry look!" The dry look still lives, despite a flirtation with greasy locks by pro basketball coach Pat Riley and inside trader Gordon Gekko. The dry look is now in its third decade. Even my father gave up hair tonic in the eighties.

The hair tonic market has fallen so far that in 1996 pharmaceutical giant Colgate-Palmolive sold off the Wildroot Creme Oil brand to a small Fort Lauderdale firm, Stephan Co. In the fifties, everyone knew the name Wildroot Creme Oil because of its saturation TV marketing: "Get Wildroot Creme Oil, Charlie; it keeps your hair in trim."

Vitalis with the V7 secret ingredient emblazoned on its bottle is a throwback to another era. If you were alive in the fifties or sixties, then you remember secret ingredients.

Vitalis with V7!

Arrid with Perstop!

Unguentine with Dianestol, the miracle pain reliever!

Preparation H with Bio-Dyne, the discovery of a world-famous research institute!

Eye-Gene with Lexatol!

Revlon Touch-and-Glo liquid makeup with Lanolite!

They were the mysterious chemicals that made our hair slicker, our teeth whiter, our underarms drier and our butts less itchy.

But it was a different era. Secrets were good, Russia was bad and CIA wasn't a four-letter word. Then came the seventies with Watergate and Cambodian incursions and open-code dating. Secrecy was out.

It's almost impossible to find a drugstore product that brays about its miracle secret ingredient anymore. We no longer care if the Russians know what's in our toothpaste. Or how our deodorant keeps us dry.

And we want to know what's in our toothpaste and our deodorant and our hemorrhoid cream. So we can look it up in a book and determine for ourselves if it is safe to roll under our arms or rub on our butts.

We can trace the explosion in secret ingredients to one event, the introduction in 1954 of Gleem with GL-70. Oh, there were secret ingredients before GL-70. Lots of them. Colgate, the number-one toothpaste at the time, had Gardol, "the invisible shield." Ipana, the number-two toothpaste, had something called WD-9.

But Gleem, with a name that promised gleaming white teeth, was a modern marketing miracle. Gleem captured 23 percent of the toothpaste market in its first eighteen months! No product before or since has had such a spectacular introduction, not even the no-fat cookies of the eighties. No one knew exactly what it was that vaulted Gleem into the toothpaste big leagues; maybe it was that spy-plane-sounding secret ingredient, GL-70, that captured the public's fancy. Or that perfect-smile name, Gleem. Or even that marvelous advertising line—"For people who can't brush after every meal." Something worked and every manufacturer would try to emulate that success formula. And one part of that formula was that mysterious-sounding secret ingredient.

So the fifties were alive with secret ingredients.

When Crest toothpaste came along in 1958, Procter & Gamble couldn't just advertise that it was fortified with stannous fluoride, a compound that had been scientifically proven in controlled experiments to reduce tooth decay. Americans weren't chemists—well, a few were, but most weren't—so they couldn't understand that stannous fluoride was but one of 150 different fluorides that had been tried in an effort to emulate the success of fluoridated drinking water in reducing tooth decay. So the marketing men at P&G put their thinking caps on. And Crest— the most effective decay-preventive dentifrice ever made—was advertised as Crest with Fluoristan.

Fluoristan was P&G's trademarked name for stannous fluoride and heat-treated orthophosphate abrasive. It would have been hard to advertise stannous fluoride and heat-treated orthophosphate abrasive. First, they would have had to find an announcer who could pronounce it. Then they would have had to explain it. Fluoristan was a short-hand ad slogan. Did Americans know what it was? No. Did they care? No. All they knew was that it sounded like a miracle secret ingredient.

Eventually Gleem and GL-70 fell by the wayside. Today it is a nonfactor in the toothpaste wars. WD-9 went to advertising heaven, along with Gardol and GL-70 and all those other secret ingredients.

Only V7 remains. On the bottom shelf. Of the smallest section in the drugstore.

The days of secret ingredients are past. So it's okay if I reveal what they really were.

Gardol is—or was—N-Methyl-N-(1-oxododecyl) glycine sodium salt. It is—or was—a detergent foaming agent with antienzyme. It was patented in 1954 by Colgate-Palmolive.

GL-70 and WD-9 were both detergents with anti-bacterial properties.

The chemical name for Lexatol, the secret ingredient in the

eyewash Eye-Gene, is phenylephrine hydrochloride. It's a blood vessel constrictor.

Bio-Dyne was a moisturizer for skin. Its main use was to minimize the dryness and pain of sunburn and wind-chapped skin. And Preparation H had you put it on your butt.

Geritol contains Ferrex 18, which the bottle identifies in small print—much too small for a Geritol consumer to read—as ferric ammonium citrate. This Ferrex 18 is quite the miracle ingredient, too. The Ohio State University Horticulture and Crop Science service says ferric ammonium citrate capsules inserted into the trunks of pin oak trees will prevent the tree disease iron chlorosis (a sort of iron-deficiency anemia for trees). And the Japan Society of Magnetic Resonance in Medicine says in a 1996 journal article that a ferric ammonium citrate–cellulose paste is great for a different use: "We conclude that this new oral contrast agent could be used routinely in MRI of the esophagus."

Perhaps the most interesting secret ingredient is V7 itself. It's not the main ingredient in Vitalis. That's alcohol, which, because of its drying power, has been a staple in hair tonic for decades.

In the fifties, Vitalis trademarked the name "V7" for trimetozine, a drug whose main use was as a sedative. That's right, if you used Vitalis hair tonic in the fifties you were smearing sedative in your hair. Now you know why you slept so well back then. Your hair tonic contained the original hair relaxant.

So what's in the modern version of Vitalis? Let's see, the main ingredient is SD alcohol 40. In other words, alcohol. That's followed by PPG-40 butyl ether, a compound derived from ethyl alcohol. In other words, alcohol.

Then there's water, which you know about, benzyl benzoate, which is a solvent used as fixative in perfumes and chewing-gum flavors, and dihydroabietyl alcohol. More alcohol. That's alcohol, alcohol, water, solvent and alcohol. No wonder winos used to drink this stuff. They knew what the *real* secret ingredient was.

Head & Shoulders—6.8-Ounce Bottle—$2.99

The legal name for dandruff is pityriasis capitis—that's if you're going to sue over it. And if you are, you might as well make it a class action lawsuit, because 40 percent of the population has dandruff.

What is dandruff? It's those white flakes that you see all over nerds' sweaters. What causes it? After years of study, scientists have finally concluded that dandruff is just overzealous cells maturing in one week instead of the usual four and migrating to the surface of the scalp, pushing the old cells off in a big giant flake.

What makes cells overzealous? We don't know. It could be they are in a hurry to get to a PTA meeting. But most scientists who study dandruff think it is a yeast-like germ called *pityrosporum orbiculare.*

And how would you like to be a scientist who studies dandruff? What do you tell your kids? Or worse, what do they tell their friends?

Thanks to these dandruff researchers, there is something you can do. You can use antidandruff shampoos, which have been around since the early sixties.

In 1955, after five years of testing, P&G researchers concluded that zinc pyrithione, a compound developed by Olin Chemical Company, could be effective in preventing dandruff. They went to scientists at Vanderbilt University, and another five years—and 1,300 tests—later they had their product. They named it "Head & Shoulders," after the area where dandruff originates and the area where it lands. It was test marketed in 1960 and introduced nationwide three years later.

How does it work? Head & Shoulders retards cell growth. The active ingredient is zinc pyrithinate, a variation on the original compound, and yes, it tingles. Is that good? Yes, that's good, because the commercials say so.

Since the success of Head & Shoulders, there have been imitators.

There are now two ways to treat dandruff. The Head & Shoulders way—to retard cell growth—and the Selsun Blue way—to remove excess cells. Selsun Blue's active ingredient is selenium sulfide. (X-Seb does the same thing with a different active ingredient, salicylic acid).

Tegrin, like Head & Shoulders, retards cell growth but does it with a different active ingredient, coal tars. Yes, coal tars can cause cancer when left on a rat's scalp for the equivalent of fifty years. But scientists say nonrats like us shouldn't worry because the tars come in contact with our scalps for such a short period of time during shampooing.

Clairol Nice 'n Easy—Light Ash Blonde—$3.39

Try this exercise: walk down the street and as you pass women count the number of blondes. Is it 10 percent, 20 percent, 30 percent? The natural incidence of blond hair is 5 percent. The artificial incidence is 40 percent. Forty percent of American women add blondness to their hair. Every blonde you passed over 5 percent is taking heed of Clairol's sixties ad: "If I had my life to live over, I'd live it as a blonde."

Blond has been in since Clairol began the hair coloring revolution in the fifties with one very clever little advertising slogan: "Isn't it true blondes have more fun?"

Suddenly every woman in America wanted to be a blonde.

Not that they announced it publicly. Hair coloring was still a closely guarded secret until the sixties. "Bottle blonde" were cat-fighting words. So Clairol followed its "blondes have more fun" campaign with a sort of whisper campaign: "Does she or doesn't she?" The implication being that Clairol hair color was so good, nobody could tell. For this to fully make sense, you have to realize that before Clairol's ads, coloring your hair blond was the same as hanging a HOOKER sign on your ass.

Blonde was synonymous with *slut,* at least in Hollywood, from which most Americans took their cues. Most stars of the thirties and forties were brunettes and redheads. Even natural blondes, like Bette Davis and Carole Lombard, darkened their hair. The blondes of moviedom were the fallen women: Mae West and Jean Harlow. (When Barbara Stanwyck played a fallen woman in *Double Indemnity* she wore a blonde wig.) In 1935, at the peak of Jean Harlow's popularity, Clairol sold only $350,000 worth of hair coloring.

When the movie *Gentlemen Prefer Blondes* came out in 1953, the title was ironic. Gentlemen didn't prefer blondes. Until they saw Marilyn Monroe in the movie. MM made blond sexy, playful and desirable.

And suddenly hair coloring took off. And much of that boom could be attributed to blond ambition. Between 1950 and 1960 sales of Clairol's blond tints jumped from 5 percent of the company's business to 20 percent.

Women had been coloring their hair since Cleopatra's day; she and her ladies used powder, henna and goat's grease for coloring. But chemical dyes weren't developed until the twentieth century. The first dyes really were that: dyes. And the results weren't pretty. They just painted the hair, giving dyed hair a harsh look.

The twenties saw a number of women bring lawsuits claiming hair dye had poisoned them or made them bald. A 1922 study by New York City's health commissioner, Dr. Royal Copeland, showed that one woman in 8,000 was allergic to the metal dyes then in use. New York passed a law requiring patch tests to determine if a woman was allergic to the dyes be conducted twenty-four hours before any hair coloring session. And soon the federal government followed suit. It was a widely ignored law.

Enter Lawrence Gelb, the future president of American Clairol. During a trip to Europe in 1931, Gelb discovered a dying process that permeated the hair shaft instead of just painting it. It wasn't a dye, and it took minutes, not hours. And, most important, it could be done at home. It was already called Clairol, and Gelb bought the American rights from the French company Mury.

Gelb brought this technique home from Europe and named it tint, to distinguish it from those horrible dyes. It was gaining popularity, but hadn't yet fully caught on. What really boomed Clairol sales was the development of a new product line. It was eight years in the making, but in 1950 Clairol introduced the one-step hair coloring kit. That year *Life* magazine estimated that only 10 million American women were tinting their hair. By the end of the decade, that number had doubled. The one-step treatment was a big part of it; but so too was that catchy little ad line dreamed up by Foote, Cone & Belding copywriter Shirley Polykoff: "Does she or doesn't she? Hair color so natural only her hairdresser knows for sure." Beauty salons in 1956 derived only 5 percent of their revenue from hair tinting. By 1961 that had jumped to 30 percent. The "Does she or doesn't she?" ad would run for two decades, a boom time for hair coloring. Clairol's sales quadrupled between 1950 and 1970.

Not that other companies weren't noticing. In 1961, Clairol's soon-to-be-archrival entered the American market. L'Oréal had long been the hair color queen of Europe. Its hair coloring process had been developed in 1907 by French chemist Eugene Schueller. He began selling it to hair salons under the brand name Aureole, which is French for "halo." When he outgrew his kitchen lab, he decided to change the brand name to the more luxurious-sounding L'Oréal, which is just a corruption of Aureole. It implies "crowning glory," according to Kathy Smith, consumer advisor at L'Oréal.

In the sixties, hair color entered the mainstream. There were ten manufacturers of hair tint in this country. Sales were booming. Women everywhere were highlighting and tinting and coloring. Then, at the end of the decade, inexplicably, hair coloring sales leveled off. (Those damned hippies! Plus, the number of women hitting middle age slowed.)

The wilderness years for hair color ended in 1992. After years of slow or no growth, hair coloring sales started picking up that year, and by 1995, *Drug Topics* magazine could call it a "long-term trend."

L'Oréal, one of the companies responsible for that long-term trend, says 43 million people colored their hair in 1993, compared to 36 million in 1991. In just two years, 7 million people who hadn't had the hair-tint habit suddenly became addicted.

What happened? Simple demographics, my friend.

The prime target group for hair color is women thirty-five and older—got to cover that gray. There are more and more of them every day as the baby boom continues its glacial march to senility.

Today, half of all American women between thirteen and seventy color their hair; that has increased by 50 percent in just the last ten years.

And it's not just baby boomers and blue-haired old ladies. Half of all new users are under thirty-five. For them, hair color is a fashion statement. L'Oréal found that 25 percent of women twelve to twenty-four color their hair.

The typical drugstore, if there is such a thing, sells almost $8,000 worth of hair tint a year. For drugstores, hair tint passed shampoo as the top-selling hair care product in 1995. How can that be? How can people color their hair more than they wash it? Dollar volume. It's more expensive than shampoo.

Like drug addiction, hair coloring starts out innocently enough. Women experiment, first with semipermanent tints and rinses such as Loving Care, then go to the hard stuff, permanent tints like Preference, Excellence and Nice 'n Easy.

Actually, the drug comparison is not that far fetched. Hair tint is like a drug: once you start you can't stop. And you have to retint about every six weeks. They should give hair color away to first-timers.

The top five hair tints in 1994 were L'Oréal Preference, Clairol Nice 'n Easy, Clairol Loving Care, L'Oréal Excellence and Clairol Ultress. Preference and Nice 'n Easy accounted for one-third of all hair color sales.

The most popular hair colors in 1997, according to category manager for Drug Emporium Joe Weingarten, were:

1. Champagne blond
2. Light brown
3. Light golden brown
4. Medium brown
5. Light ash blond

That national trend is pretty much mirrored at a beauty parlor down the street from me. At Z-Salon & Spa in Louisville, Kentucky, the top five hair colors are:

1. Towhead blond—"Baby boomers are trying to revert back to when they were younger and they are trying to have children's hair," says color and texture studio manager Lisa Strader.
2. Honey blonde—"Clients want to look natural and they're reverting back to younger days when they spent the entire summer outside."
3. Chestnut brown—"People with dark hair are trying to take the hardness out."
4. Golden red—"We don't do a lot of the fluorescent red."
5. Ash brown—"This is for people going gray who don't want reds in their hair."

Clairol's "blondes have more fun" campaign may have made hair coloring a national passion, but it was L'Oréal's "because I'm worth it" that made it a national obsession. And while L'Oréal was charging into the market, Clairol was losing its focus and its market share. From 1976 to 1987, Clairol had seven presidents and lost its death grip on the hair color market.

Clairol is still number one, but L'Oréal is a closing number two. Of the $2 billion American hair color market in 1996, Clairol and L'Oréal combined for 90 percent. Clairol once had a 66 percent share. That's now down to 47 percent. In the past decade, L'Oréal has increased its share from 24 percent to 43 percent. Revlon, the low-end company, is third with 6 percent. But in drugstores, Revlon is beloved. It holds an 8 percent share in drugstores, but because the company has not engaged in price cutting, it is the most profitable hair color line for the stores.

Of course, drugstore owners love hair color, period. They call it a "basket builder." For every box of hair coloring that is sold, the drugstore sells another forty dollars' worth of cosmetics, shampoos and conditioners.

Druggists aren't the only ones who profit from hair color. Everyone in the hair tint food chain makes money. But especially the manufacturers. The key ingredients in hair color are cheap: peroxide, ammonia and pigment. The finished product sells for four to ten dollars, a 70 percent gross profit.

And Coke thinks it's got a good deal because it can get a buck for a bottle of sugar water.

Grecian Formula 16—2-Ounce Bottle—$7.29

I had my high school reunion this summer, and two days before I left to go back home, I looked in the mirror and considered using Grecian Formula. Only for a split second and only in passing. But I considered it. I'm sure my father never once thought about coloring his gray hair. My mother . . . that's a different story.

The hair coloring story is a changing one.

Men's hair coloring is where women's hair coloring was in the fifties: in the closet. If I had dyed my hair for the reunion, I sure as hell wouldn't have told anyone. Not even my wife. (Because she would have told everyone.) Women talk openly about the shade of hair coloring they use. Men don't talk about it, period.

Yet American men purchased $100 million worth of hair tint in 1996. Granted, that's only one-twentieth of what American women spent on hair color. And of the amount men spent, about one-third was spent on women's products. "Just getting it for the little woman. Honest. It's not for me. I swear it." Still, one in eight American men over thirty-five dyes his hair, twice as many as ten years ago. Combe Inc., with Just for Men and Grecian Formula 16, dominates, with a 75 percent market share.

How does Grecian formula know what color your hair used to be? It doesn't. It gradually puts color pigment back in your hair. When you reach your natural color, you stop using it as often.

Aqua Net Hair Spray, Extra Super Hold—7-Ounce Can—$1.39

Big hair, the much-mocked trailer-park look, has its origins in the seventies . . . the 1770s. That's when men powdered and poofed their wigs as high as possible. These macaronis, as they were called (it was their favorite food), wore small hats for much the same reason that the big-haired trailer-park women of today drive small cars—to accentuate the big-hair look. Women of the colonial period followed suit, adding to the look by inserting baubles, plumes, ribbons, lace, even fruit into their hair. And you thought country music stars had funny hairdos.

With the French Revolution, it was off with their heads and off with their big hair. But big hair made a comeback at the turn of the twentieth century, soon replaced by the bob. In the early sixties it took the form of the beehive, a brief teen fad. (And perhaps a reaction to the pompadours and jellyrolls that were favored by greaser boys in the late fifties.)

Dolly Parton led a brief resurgence, at least among her fans, of big hair in the early seventies. But then it made its big comeback with the big, untamed Farrah Fawcett look of the late seventies. It's been popular somewhere ever since.

How do women get and keep that mile-high look? Hair spray. How does hair spray do it? Once it did it the old-fashioned way—it glued your hair down. Originally, hair spray was lacquer. Real lacquer. Today it is mostly alcohol, which dries the hair out, making it stiff.

Prell Shampoo—15-Ounce Bottle—$3.49

Before 1934 folks washed their hair—"worshed" was actually the more typical pronunciation for most hair washers—with bathroom soap. Then came Drene. The oddly named liquid shampoo was a spin-off from Dreft liquid dishwashing detergent, but a spin-off in the same way that *The Facts of Life* was a spin-off from *Diff'rent Strokes,* related but nothing really alike.

Drene was first marketed to beauty parlors, then, in 1936, to drugstores. It marked the first time Procter & Gamble had ever marketed to drugstores, and as Rick said to Captain Renault in *Casablanca,* "I think this is the beginning of a beautiful friendship." P&G products are now a drugstore staple.

Drene was a stunning success. People liked the fact that they didn't have to scrub their hair with a bar of soap, the same way they scrubbed their underarms. This Drene stuff was, like, luxurious.

Just one problem. It worked too well. Not only did it cleanse hair of dirt, it also removed all the natural oils, leaving Mom with clean, straw-like shafts on her head. A quick trip back to the lab and the addition of a conditioning agent corrected all that.

The success of Drene caused P&G to build an in-house beauty salon and give free treatments to employees. It was a great benefit, except for the fact that someone at the plant got the bright idea to test out new products on the employees. This usually involved the two-sided shampoo, right side with a leading brand, left side with new Something or Other. A new concept was born: the bad half-hair day.

Drene was followed and soon supplanted by Prell in 1946.

Prell came in a tube, and the radio commercials featured Tallulah the Tube screeching, "Take me home and squeeze me." Of course Hollywood star Tallulah Bankhead sued, claiming, "I'm the only person ever named Tallulah." She asked for a million dollars in damages. There were no damages. How could there be damages? Her career had been dead for years. But the resulting publicity rejuvenated her career and gave Prell millions in free publicity. In the end she settled, quietly, out of court for $2,500.

And Procter & Gamble had a new partner: the nation's druggists.

5
The Face:
The Place Is the Cosmetics Case

Tylenol may be the number-one product in the drugstore, but numbers two, three and four are Revlon cosmetics, Cover Girl cosmetics and Maybelline cosmetics. And so it is that cosmetics are king—or queen—in the drugstore. Drugstores are the place for your face.

Cover Girl Lipstick—Brandyberry Color—$4.98

There are two kinds of cosmetics: class and mass. "Class" are the high-end perfumes and powders and lip glosses sold in department and specialty stores. "Mass" are the mass-market items, aimed at budget-minded women and sold in discount outlets and drugstores. You won't find Chanel No. 5 in the pharmacy. Why would you look for it here anyway?

The drugstore and the cosmetics counter seem an unlikely combination. No one makes any serious health claims for most cosmetics. (Lipstick may inhibit chapped lips, but fingernail polish doesn't strengthen nails, despite claims to the effect.)

So how did drugstores end up in the cosmetics business? For that answer, let's turn to the 1948 edition of *Remington's Practice of Pharmacy*. Drugstores carry other merchandise, Remington explained, as a "natural outgrowth of the practice of pharmacy," making these goods, as well as regular pharmacy items available "in many communities which would otherwise have had to do without them."

Grandma couldn't have had lipstick on the prairie if not for good ol' Doc Johnson, the friendly pharmacist. According to Remington, "The demarcation between preparations which are for beautification and those which are used for the relief of human ailments is neither sharp nor paramount."

In other words, Doc sold whatever sold.

Maybelline Great Lash Mascara—$2.98

So who is this Maybelline anyway? The same chick who showed up in the Chuck Berry song? Probably not. The Maybelline of Maybelline was actually named Mabel—Mabel Williams. And she was sitting on her bed in the Chicago boardinghouse room she shared with her brother, minding her own business and applying her homemade mascara when her brother T. L. started watching. He was fascinated at how well her mix of petroleum jelly and black pigment worked. He decided to add this product to his mail-order catalog. He originally called it "Lash-Brow-Ine" but when that didn't sell, renamed it for his sister Mabel: Mabel-ine, which became Maybelline. The rest is mascara history.

Lady Stetson Perfume—1-Ounce Bottle—$16.00

Perfumery isn't the oldest profession—we all know what that is—but it is one of the oldest crafts. And members of the oldest profession often rely on the perfumer to increase their business.

The basic techniques of the modern perfumer are pretty much the same as those of Egyptian perfumers of four millennia ago: selecting fragrant oils and blending them into something that smells like Elizabeth Taylor or Cher or Jaclyn Smith or whomever.

Humans have always liked pleasant aromas. Incense has been used in virtually every human culture. The Greek philosopher Plutarch wrote about the ancient Egyptian perfume kyphi—and he could just as easily have been writing about the latest trendy fragrance: "Its aromatic substances lull to sleep, allay anxieties, and brighten dreams. It is made of things that delight most in the night."

Ancient Egyptians used oils and unguents for both spiritual and medicinal purposes five thousand years ago. Even earlier than that, civilizations used burnt aromatic herbs and woods to drive out evil spirits. The Oracle at Delphi inhaled the smoke from burning bay leaves to induce a trance that enabled him to communicate with the gods. In the Old Testament, God taught Moses how to create a holy perfume, based on frankincense, myrrh and exotic gums. And Moses took eight incense ingredients with him during the Exodus: styrax, ladanum, galbanum, frankincense, myrrh, sweet cinnamon, cassia and sweet cane.

But enough about how ancients enjoyed aromas. We still do.

A 1988 study by J. Byrne-Quinn demonstrated that a person's scent ranks high when it comes to first impressions. The researcher asked 800 American women which of a number of personal attributes they noticed about people on first meeting. Some 43 percent cited scent, slightly more than picked face, eyes and voice, but fewer than hair, dress, skin and hands. (Hands? American women notice hands during an introduction?)

But scent isn't out there interacting in a vacuum, as a 1984 study at Purdue University demonstrated. In this study by R. A. Baron, a research assistant put two drops of Jungle Gardenia, the schoolgirl perfume of the sixties, behind each ear and was then introduced to male undergraduate subjects. The subjects were then asked if they liked this scented young woman. Their reactions depended on what she was wearing. If she was dressed casually, they were ready to jump bones. But if she was in formal business clothes, they saw her as conceited. The lesson, I guess, is if you are meeting new people and you are dressed in your dungarees, then by all means wear perfume. But if you are dressed up, scent won't help; they'll still think you are stuck up.

It is not true that people with big noses have better senses of smell than those with small proboscises. If it were, all the perfumers of the world would look like W. C. Fields or Jimmy Durante. And they don't.

We don't actually smell with our noses but with the olfactory receptors that are located inside at the top of the nose. There are about fifty million of them, give or take five, but they would all fit on a postage stamp.

The average life of one of these cells is about a month. Because there are so many receptors, you can smell an odor with as few as seven or eight molecules. Which explains the silent-but-deadly theory of flatulence. It only takes seven silent molecules.

While Tylenol will top the list of best-selling analgesics for ten years in a row, the best-selling women's fragrances change almost annually. The top five fragrances of 1995, the latest year for which there are figures, were:

Vanderbilt, with sales of $32.8 million.
Jovan—$30.8 million
Exclamation—$27.7 million
Lady Stetson—$23.3 million
Navy—$23 million

Topaz Golden Spice—$2.39

The fastest-burgeoning section in the drugstore? Burgeon, burgeon, burgeon. You've found it: cosmetics for African-American women.

The African-American woman has gone from being the invisible woman to the woman of the hour, and in the process, the drugstore's cosmetics section for African-American women has taken off. As recently as 1989, there were only a handful of small companies making cosmetics for African-American women. The whole section was a couple of feet wide. It has exploded in the nineties as the cosmetics industry awakened to women of color. And the color was green. African-American women spend $4 billion a year on cosmetics and they aren't interested in looking like Cindy Crawford.

So, suddenly, in 1992, Cover Girl had a new cover girl,

African-American model Lana Ogilvie. Revlon had a new
African-American supermodel spokeswoman, Veronica Webb.
And drugstore staples like Maybelline introduced products
aimed at ethnic women.

But the watershed moment for cosmetics for African-American women had come a year earlier, in 1991, when Estee
Lauder, the premier cosmetics line in this country, introduced
cosmetics in darker tones to their high-end department store
lines, including Prescriptives All Skins, with 115 custom-
blended shades. What made this so shocking wasn't just that
Estee Lauder was long identified with white women, but that it
was also long identified with wealthy, refined white women.
This move was belated recognition from the company that
African-American women could also be refined and wealthy. In
addition to launching Prescriptives, Estee Lauder expanded its
flagship line into darker shades and added the Color Deeps line
to its Clinique brand.

It was more than just a smart move, it was a natural. There
are 16 million African-American women in this country, one-
third of them in the prime cosmetics purchasing ages between
eighteen and thirty-four. And the drugstore was a natural place
to further this charge into a previously ignored market because,
according to Procter & Gamble research, 53 percent of sales of
cosmetics for African-American women are in the mass-market
sector.

And it is in the drugstore lines where the most intense beauty
battle for the African-American consumer is being waged. All
the names are involved, from traditional cosmetics companies
for white women like Maybelline and Revlon to traditional
African-American cosmetics companies like Flori Roberts and
Fashion Fair.

Fashion Fair, the number-one class line for African-American women, is manufactured by Johnson Products, a company that was founded in 1954 by an African-American man, George Johnson, to manufacture Ultra Wave, a hair straightener for men. It broke into the retail market in 1960 with its Ultra Sheen line of hair-care products.

Flori Roberts was founded by a white woman in 1965.

The first shot in the African-American mass-market cosmetics war was fired in 1991 when Procter & Gamble's Maybelline introduced Shades of You, which claimed to be a brand-new approach to cosmetics for African Americans. Maybelline said it wasn't just taking its same old makeup formula and making it browner. It was a new formula that reduced the titanium dioxide, a chemical that makes darker skin tones ashy-looking. Johnson entered the war the next year with a mass-market line called Ebone. Flori Roberts followed suit and soon cosmetics for African Americans were everywhere. In August 1992, Revlon entered the fray with ColorStyle.

Before the war began, Posner Laboratories controlled more than half the market. But things got interesting when Maybelline immediately grabbed a one-third market share, according to the market research firm Towne-Oller & Associates. ColorStyle landed another 5 percent. Posner lost an immediate 14 percent and the war was on.

It's still war; it's just that some of the warriors are retrenching. In 1993, IVAX, Flori Roberts's parent company, negotiated a merger with Johnson, bringing together two of the best-known lines. Then the next year the merged companies acquired Posner.

Posner is an old company; it's been in business for thirty-five years. But that pales next to the Walker Company.

If all women knew the story of Madam C. J. Walker, they might not buy any other cosmetics brand. When she was rebuffed in her attempt to attend the all-male National Negro Business League convention in 1912, she went anyway. And on the last day of the assembly, she addressed the convention. She told her story, of rising from cotton picker to hair-care millionaire, and the group was so impressed that they invited her back the next year as keynote speaker.

Born Sarah Breedlove on a Louisiana cotton plantation shortly after the end of the Civil War, she moved to St. Louis in 1904 and briefly worked selling Annie Turnbo Pope Malone's hair-care products. She had been drawn to them by Malone's "Wonderful Hair Grower," a cream designed to aid what was then a major problem among African-American women, baldness brought on by poor diet and damaging hair treatments. Breedlove decided to develop her own hair-care products. She moved to Denver in 1906, married a newspaper sales agent named C. J. Walker—and christened herself Madam, in the manner of many businesswomen of her day: Madam C. J. Walker.

Her first product, a hair-growing elixir, came to her in a dream. She told *Literary Digest* in 1917, "A big black man appeared to me (in a dream) and told me what to mix up for my hair. Some of the remedy was grown in Africa, but I sent for it, mixed it, put it on my scalp, and in a few weeks my hair was coming in faster than it had ever fallen out."

She is generally credited with inventing the hot comb for straightening hair, although it is more likely she adapted the

French hot curling iron and popularized it in the African-American community. She believed her hot comb was more natural than Annie Malone's hair-pulling technique. Madam Walker moved her company to Indianapolis in 1910 to take advantage of that city's central location and eight railway connections. By 1916, the Walker Company had 20,000 sales agents, and Madam C. J. Walker was America's first African-American female millionaire, and perhaps its first self-made female millionaire.

Ivory Soap—3.5-Ounce Bars, Four-Pack—$1.38

The most famous name in the drugstore is also the oldest. Procter & Gamble, makers of Pampers and Crest and Old Spice, was founded more than a century and a half ago in Cincinnati by William Procter and James Gamble.

It was—appropriately enough—a need for a drugstore that brought them both to the Queen City. Gamble's parents were actually heading west to Illinois, but young James started retching on an Ohio riverboat and they stopped at the nearest town for medicine. The nearest town was Cincinnati and they never left it.

Procter's father had gone broke in Britain and the family came to the New World for a new start. They too were heading west, but only to Louisville, when William's mother came down with cholera. The nearest medicine was in, you guessed it, Cincinnati. And thus were Procter & Gamble and Cincinnati eternally wed.

They didn't begin as drug vendors. Their first ad, in the June

29, 1838, edition of the *Cincinnati Gazette,* was for something
else:

> Oil for lamps and machinery. A fine article of clarified
> Pig's Foot Oil, equal to sperm, at a low price and in
> quantities to suit buyers. Neat's Foot oil ditto. Also No.
> 1 & 2 soap, Palm and shaving ditto. For sale by Procter
> & Gamble Co., east side Main Street 2nd door off 6th
> Street.

They were just trying to start a business using by-products from
Cincinnati's thriving meat-rending industries.

In 1879, they began manufacturing a white soap they called
Ivory. They made it in a sort of giant mixing machine. The
mixer's attendant determined when it was ready to be poured
into molds. One day he went to lunch and left the machine running. When he came back, it had overflowed. He didn't want to
get in trouble, so he went ahead and poured it into the molds
and went on about his business. Weeks later, P&G began getting
orders for that "soap that floats." No one had a clue what the
customers meant until the worker, whose name has been lost, remembered his screwup. From then on, Ivory soap was whipped
up so it would float.

Harley Procter, William's son, wanted a "pure" soap, but
there was no definition of pure when it came to soap. So he con-
sulted an independent scientist, who said soap should be all fatty
acids and alkali. Anything else would be "foreign and unnecessary substances."

Procter had Ivory analyzed at an independent lab. The result:
the only "foreign and unnecessary substances" were "uncom-
bined alkali 0.11%, carbonates 0.28% and mineral matter

0.17%." A little math and Harley had it. Ivory was "99 and 44/100ths percent pure." And the slogan stuck. For years. And years. It's still on the bar.

Harley was quite the innovator. He was also responsible for naming Ivory. He was in church one Sunday when he was thunderstruck by a bit of scripture: "And thy garments smell of myrrh, aloes, and cassia, out of ivory palaces whereby they have made thee glad." That was it. What had previously been known around P&G as the White soap, became on that day Ivory. (Good thing the reverend wasn't in Revelations that Sunday; no telling what the name might have been.)

Camay beauty soap hit the market in 1923, the first time any company had ever created a product to compete with its own existing product, in this case, Ivory soap. But the Procters and the Gambles weren't gambling. They knew that if they didn't introduce their own hard-milled perfumed soap, competitors' brands would steal from Ivory. Better to steal from yourself than to allow your competitors to. And that's a business slogan we can all live with.

Neutrogena—3.5-Ounce Bar—$2.49

Cringe when you see a three-dollar bar of soap? Well, this is the mother of all those designer soaps. Developed in Belgium in 1954 by Dr. Edward Fromont, Neutrogena was created to be less irritating to the skin. It sold for a dollar a bar in the fifties, when many soaps were ten cents each. And it has continued to sell at premium prices, either because Americans want a premium soap that you can see through, or because there's one born every minute.

Clearasil—1-Ounce Tube—$5.79

To squeeze or not to squeeze, that is the question. Or, at least, it's the question posed by teenagers since time began. Should they pop that pimple? Or let it run its course?

For many, the latter is unthinkable: My god! A zit on my heretofore perfect skin! The former is bad for the complexion and can cause hideous scars that are worse than zits because they last to eternity. There must be a middle ground. And in the drugstore, you can find it—the skin-toned acne cream that fights the zit while covering it up.

Skin-toned acne creams were invented in the fifties when teenagers first officially roamed the earth. (The word *teenager* was coined in 1955 by Dick Clark, to describe how he wanted to look in forty years.) But because everyone has a different skin tone, Clearasil, perhaps not wanting to offend anybody, created a skin-toned product that was the tone of no one's skin. What it was was a giant billboard that pointed to the zit on your chin.

Advances in zit control have pretty much pulled Clearasil back into the pack—and put dermatologists into Mercedeses. The over-the-counter product of choice today is benzoyl peroxide, the active ingredient in a half-hundred zit creams, from Acetoxyl to Zeroxin. Clearasil has benzoyl peroxide too, and it still sells, but it's not the fashion statement it was in the sixties. Oxy-5 and Oxy-10, with their chemical crime-fighting names, are tops.

Coppertone—4-Ounce Bottle—$5.49

You would think that the thousands of articles and news reports about the dangers of getting a tan, skin cancer and all that, would have killed the suntan industry, right? Think again. In 1996, Americans spent $1 billion in tanning salons and another $393.5 million on suntan lotions. Admittedly, some of that lotion dollar could be classified as "health care"—dollars spent to avoid getting a tan.

But a 1991 study by a Wake Forest University professor found that 90 percent of college students "caught some rays" at least occasionally to enhance their tan. And a whopping 12 percent thought that they could never get tan enough.

Maybe this shouldn't surprise us. Not in a nation where young vegetarians smoke two packs a day.

In the drugstore, it's called the sun-care market, and the name in sun-care products is Coppertone. In fact, Coppertone has been the name in suntan lotions since the days when every other billboard on the beach featured that pesky dog nipping at that little girl's ass, er, swimsuit, pulling it down enough to show her suntan line. Almost 40 percent of all suntan lotions sold are Coppertone, a market share that's held since the days when the prime competitor was Sea & Ski.

Sea & Ski once pulled even with Coppertone in the sixties, each with 38 percent of the market. But Sea & Ski has fallen off the chart and given way to "sunscreens." Second on the top tan is PreSun, with about 12 percent. Banana Boat ranks third at 8.2 percent, a tan-line tenth above Shade, which has 8.1 percent of the market. Bain de Soleil is fifth, at 6.6 percent. Another one-time coulda-been-a-contender, Hawaiian Tropic, ranks seventh, with 5.7 percent. Sea & Ski, the "tan-fastic" lotion, doesn't chart.

Sunscreens work on an amazingly simple proposition: they block out UV rays, the sun's bad-boy rays, and are rated by how successful they block these rays. A sun protection factor (SPF) of 0 means no protection. You will fry in the sun there, whitey. It goes on up to 50, although sun scientists say that for all practical purposes an 18 means no UV rays get through. The number means a tan that would normally take you one hour to achieve will require three hours with an SPF of 3. The degree of blocking you need depends on your skin tone and how much tan you want. White people have a natural SPF of 0. They need sunscreen. According to the folks at Coppertone, the average African-American person has a natural SPF of 8. So they too need some sunscreen.

How do they know that a sunblock product works? They test it. Where do they test it? This is a trick question. Go ahead and guess. The Bahamas? The tan-test subjects wish. You can guess Daytona and Myrtle Beach, Fort Lauderdale and Destin, and you still won't be close. Schering-Plough Health Care, manufacturers of Coppertone suntan lotion and Dr. Scholl's corn plasters, test their sun-fun skin-care products in Memphis, Tennessee. Why? They get varying weather conditions there. In the beach resort towns all they get is heat and sun. And while that is one of the prime conditions for a sunscreen, it's not the only one.

Coppertone was invented by a pharmacist, Miami Beach drugstore owner Benjamin Green. Green had noticed the myriad homemade concoctions that tourists were rubbing on their skins to prevent sunburn and decided to see if he couldn't come up with a prepackaged product. He cooked cocoa butter in his wife's coffee pot and tested it on his own bald head. It worked! In 1944 he sold what he called Coppertone Suntan Cream in bottles with a picture of an Indian chief saying, "Don't be a paleface." Ah, the days before political correctness.

Barbasol Shave Cream—4-Ounce Tube—$1.39

From the forgotten but not gone file comes Barbasol. They still make it and they still sell it. It's just that the "beard buster," as it's always been called, doesn't have the marketing power it once did. But it's still sold in the same kind of tube it was sold in when it first hit the market in 1920.

And it's still one of the leading shave creams in the country, according to Stuart Bauer, marketing manager of Pfizer Inc. It's just that shave cream is not the product category it was in 1920, in the pre–aerosol can days, when Grandpa hung his mirror on a tree, sharpened his razor on the strop, swirled Barbasol in his shaving cup until it foamed, and proceeded to do one of the most amazing shaving jobs any little kid could imagine. All without a nick or a cut.

Barbasol is a wonderful old-fashioned kind of name, the sort of name you know was coined in an earlier day. "Barb" from barber and "ol" because that was a popular product suffix of that bygone era: Bisodol, Pepto-Bismol, Lysol. (The "as" was to give the name a little lilt; "Barbol" would have sounded too much like Ollie and his wife Barb.)

"The beard buster" catchphrase is still on the tube. In fact, it's still the same Barbasol. "We still market the original product that we've been marketing for seventy-seven years," says Bauer, who noted that it's still the same target audience, too. "It's men with beards, a general male population kind of product. Men twenty to eighty . . . I'm picking these numbers out of a hat. There was no market research back then."

Kleenex—175-Tissue Box—$1.28

Anyone who has ever written for a newspaper has probably experienced this: a letter arrives unannounced in your work mailbox, with one of those Horton, Morton and Wharton–type return addresses. Open it, and inside is a mildly threatening letter, reminding the writer that Kleenex® is a registered trademark of Kimberly-Clark and when using it in a story, it should be capitalized with that little ® symbol. Yeah, right, I'm going to try and figure out where that little ® symbol is on my keyboard.

Well, it almost happened to Kleenex, their lawyers' worst fears. Kleenex® almost became Kleenex. The point is, Kleenex is such a well-known brand that it is in jeopardy of being genericized, if that's a word. It will become a generic, meaning folks will use the words *Kleenex* and *facial tissue* interchangeably and Kimberly-Clark will lose its trademark. It's already happened to Aspirin and Cellophane, so the brands that have held on to their trademarks are vigilant about defending them.

The positive side of this, or it should be a positive, is that people identify Kleenex and facial tissue so closely that the latter has become the former. That has to help sales, doesn't it? "Honey, when you're down at the store, could you pick up a box of Kleenex?" Notice: not Puffs. Not a box of Generic Facial Tissues. But Kleenex.

When people think about blowing their nose, they think Kleenex. And that has to be good.

It didn't start that way. When Kleenex made its debut in 1924, it was called the "disposable cold cream towel."

An ad in the April 1925 issue of *Picture-Play* magazine trumpeted, "The secret of famous stage beauties is simply the use of

Kleenex in removing cold cream and cosmetics. This soft, vel-vet absorbent is made of cellucotton. Use it once, throw it away." Nice idea, disposable cold cream towel, but not a great idea. Women need to wipe off cold cream maybe once a day.

The great idea came in 1930 when the company changed its ads and began calling Kleenex "the disposable handkerchief." And today it really is *the* disposable handkerchief.

Gillette Sensor Razor—$2.98

It was a king who popularized shaving in Europe. And it was a King who popularized the habit in America. King Charles II convinced his lords that a gentleman needed a smooth face, free of whiskers. And King Gillette, a Massachusetts man with five o'clock shadow and a dull straight razor, made the custom an American tradition. Gillette was shaving with his old straight ra-zor one summer morning in 1895—or more precisely, he was dragging a dull blade across his face, nicking the skin and barely cutting the stubble—when he had a brainstorm. Why not a thin blade on a handle?

During the next six years, he was told over and over by neighboring toolmakers that it couldn't be done.

Finally he found a believer in machinist William Nickerson. Together they worked out the details of the "safety razor," a han-dle with removable blades. They bought an ad in the October 1903 issue of *System* magazine and sat back and waited for the profits to roll in. They had to wait for some time. In its first three months on the market, Gillette and Nickerson sold only 51 ra-zors and 168 blades. But you can't keep a good idea down. And in 1905, just two years later, the company sold 250,000 razors and 1.2 million blades.

What really put Gillette on the map came during World War I when the army, hearing that French soldiers had remained clean-shaven in battle by using Gillette's safety razor, ordered 3 million razors and 36 million blades. All those American doughboys over there came home with the shaving habit and Gillette was the name they had to have.

It still is: two of every three safety razors sold in this country are made by Gillette.

Rogaine Update, One Month Later

It was Day 9 of my Great Rogaine Experiment when I first heard it: "I think your hair is growing back. How long have you been using that stuff?"

"Nine days," I said. What I didn't say was that I had forgotten to spray it on for about half of those nine days.

Another friend also noticed some long hairs, evidence, she thought, that Rogaine was working: "It's not a lot. Mostly it just makes your hair look unruly. But there's definitely more hair."

Only nine days into the experiment and my friends were already noticing a difference. They still are. It is now one month in. I'm the one who lives under this chrome dome and I'm the only one who hasn't seen any hair growth.

Why are so many people seeing hair where I don't? Same reason that 11 percent of the people in

Rogaine's early tests grew hair even though they were given a placebo, not Rogaine: We see what we want to see.

I call it the Fat Vince Effect. I've been experiencing it for about twenty years, or ever since my metabolism slowed down but my eating habits didn't. Here's how it works: Every time I see a friend that I haven't seen for a long time, they always—AL-WAYS—ask me, "Have you lost weight?" For years I never understood it. Then one day it came to me in a flash of brilliance: People think I am fatter than I really am. In memory I am a fat guy. Then, when they see me and see that I am not as fat as they remembered, they assume I must have lost weight. I haven't. I haven't lost weight in seven years.

6
The Mouth:
Through the Lips and Over the Tongue, Look Out Stomach, Here I Come

The mouth is more than just the exit ramp for the voice, it is the entrance for many things: pills, toothpaste, mouthwash and cold viruses.

As Julius Caesar wrote, cold medicines as a whole are divided into three parts. No, that was Gaul he was writing about. But he could just as easily have been writing about cold medicines. Druggists divide cold medicines into three categories: cold tablets and cough drops; cold and allergy liquids; and cough syrup.

It is a huge category, one of the biggest in the drugstore in terms of dollars. The cold tablet category alone accounted for $2 billion in sales in 1996. Compare that to the gross national product of say, Greenland. I'll do it for you. The GNP of Greenland in 1996 was $500 million. That means we have more colds than Greenland has country.

Cold and allergy liquids were good for more than half a billion dollars in sales. That's nothing to sneeze at. Or maybe it is—that's half a *billion*. That's still way more than Greenland.

Even cough syrup, the stepchild of the category, accounted

for just a hair less than $400 million. Okay, Greenland did beat cough syrup.

We've got some runny noses in this country. And runny noses send us running not to the discount house or the supermarket, but to the drugstore. Pharmacies finished first in each of the three cough and cold remedies segments in sales. When we need a cold medicine, we think drugstore. This has always been a top category because coughs and colds have been with us since time immemorial and the forest primeval.

Why do we call it a cold? Or even a common cold? The name comes from the long-held assumption that the cold is caused by exposure to cold. It isn't, although that can certainly kick up the symptoms. It's caused by a virus, which is doctor talk for "we don't know what causes it."

Vicks VapoRub—1.5-Ounce Jar—$3.89

The state of North Carolina has made three major contributions to twentieth-century culture: Michael Jordan, who was born in Wilmington; Pepsi-Cola, which was born in New Bern; and Vicks VapoRub, which was born in Selma. And two of the three were created by pharmacists. (We don't think a pharmacist had anything to do with Michael's creation.)

Vicks was developed in 1905 as an alternative to the herbal vapor products that were popular at the time. Selma druggist Lunsford Richardson set out to create a salve that would offer the pain-relieving benefits of menthol without the dangers of breathing hot steam. He mixed menthol and some other chemicals in petroleum jelly and—voilà—Vicks VapoRub.

My father apparently didn't know that Vicks was created specifically so that small children wouldn't be subjected to the potential dangers of hot steam. Whenever I came down with a cold, he would set up a hot plate next to my bed, heat up a pan of water and then spoon a dab of Vicks into the water. I spent many a winter night leaning out of my bed, breathing in that hot Vicks steam. When I was sufficiently drenched in steam and sweat, he would rub Vicks on my throat, then pin a sock around my neck.

It worked.

So how did Lunsford Richardson come to invent a salve called *Vicks* VapoRub? He first called it Richardson's Croup and Pneumonia Cure Salve. Recognizing that at some time in the future someone would invent television and that his brand name would be too long for a thirty-second commercial, he renamed it to honor his brother-in-law, Dr. Joshua Vick, who had given him his first job in pharmacy and who had loaned him his back room for his VapoRub experiments.

Richardson did something that may have had a bigger impact than inventing Vicks VapoRub. He convinced the post office to let him blanket homes with free samples without having to label each package with the individual name and address. He mailed each jar to "Boxholder." In time "Boxholder" would give way to the more personal "Occupant." And thus would be born Junk Mail.

Listerine—12-Ounce Bottle—$5.19

We are not the first culture to worry about our breath odor. Far from it. Hippocrates, who lived so long ago we don't even know how to pronounce his name anymore, had his own recipe to prevent halitosis: a concoction of anise seed, myrrh and white wine.

The ancient Greeks invented a mouthwash of earthworms suspended in vinegar—and you thought tequila with one worm was gross. And to strengthen the gums, they gargled urine. Yes, urine. Particularly valued by patrician women of the time—so valued it was kept on the dressing table in an expensive onyx bottle—was the urine of an "innocent boy." Is this where Listerine got its color?

Listerine, despite its suspicious color and dreadful mediciney taste, is the number-one mouthwash in America, with a 19.2 percent market share. Americans bought $356 million worth of the stuff. Scope, with a more pleasant taste and a much prettier color, is a close second with an 18.6 percent share.

Listerine is, if nothing else, a tribute to its inventors. It was not originally created as a mouthwash. It was invented in 1879 by Dr. Joseph Lawrence and Jordan Wheat as a surgical antiseptic. They named it Listerine to honor the British doctor Sir Joseph Lister, who performed the first antiseptic surgery in 1864. In 1895 they offered it to the dental profession. And in 1914 it became one of the first products to switch from prescription to over-the-counter. It has adapted with the times. Except for the color and the taste, which remain the same: ugh!

Okay, Listerine's manufacturers have noticed a certain, uh, resistance to the trademark taste and have come up with Listerine Cool Mint. This cool idea is a hit, with a 14.3 percent market share, good for third place. Rounding out the mouthwash top five are Plax, with 8.6 percent, Chloraseptic, with 4.1 percent, and Cepacol, with 2.2 percent.

Crest Toothpaste—2.7-Ounce Tube—$2.19

Harry Day is easing his Chevy into a faculty parking lot on Indiana University's Bloomington campus. He wants to show me where it all started, where Crest toothpaste, the first effective decay-preventive dentifrice (when used in a conscientiously applied program of oral hygiene and regular professional care) and the most successful toothpaste of all time, was born. And even though the chemistry building, where it all got started, has been renovated beyond recognition since those days, Day thinks it will be instructive to visit the spot.

As he turns into a parking space, he smacks the brake. "I can't park here," he says, backing his car out of the handicapped spot. Ninety-year-old Harry Day doesn't have a handicapped sticker. Or need one.

The history of toothpaste can be divided into two periods: Before Crest and After Crest. And Harry Day bridges those two periods. It was in his dental biochemistry class in 1945 that a young Joe Muhler sat on the front row, intrigued by Dr. Day's stories of fluoride and the promise it showed for fighting tooth decay.

Harry Day helped invent the toothpaste that inspired one of the most famous slogans in advertising history: "Look, Ma, no cavities."

Crest toothpaste was born at Indiana University a half century ago, and Dr. Harry Day was present at the creation. But we are getting ahead of ourselves.

Tooth decay has plagued mankind as long as there has been a

mankind. Fourteen percent of Stone Age skulls recovered have cavities. The ancient Greeks were the first to use regular professional care, long before the Crest ads advised it. The Greeks had a special caste of slaves whose jobs were to clean their masters' mouths. These proto–dental hygienists used sticks from an evergreen tree to clean the teeth, scrubbing with powders made from common ingredients. Among the most popular tooth cleansers were powders of pumice stone, burnt eggshell or, the most popular, burnt stag horn. Mixed in for taste were bay leaves, myrrh and nightshade.

The super rich—the Aristotle Onassises of their day—preferred something a little more upscale. They liked powders made from the burnt heads of mice and from the livers of lizards. Maybe that's why they didn't call those early teeth cleaners *hygienists.*

Over time, toothpaste evolved. Thankfully.

Commercial toothpastes were available in the mid-1800s. These early toothpastes were nothing more than baking soda and soap mixed together into a paste as thick as spackle and packed in porcelain jars. Each member of the household dipped his or her toothbrush into the community paste. If you were a bachelor in New York, this was no problem. But if you were a farm boy growing up in a family of twelve, this was not too cool. In fact it was pretty nasty, all that common dipping. In 1896, a Connecticut dentist named Tracy Sheffield advanced the cause of oral hygiene when he began packaging toothpaste in a collapsible tube, an idea his son brought back from Europe, where collapsible tin tubes were used as food containers.

He started out buying the tubes from Europe, then bought his own tube-making machine. In 1892, he closed his dental practice and set up a toothpaste company. Samuel Colgate took Sheffield's idea and in 1896 ran with it. And toothpaste hasn't been packaged in porcelain jars since. But back to the story of Harry Day.

Harry Day arrived on the IU campus in 1940, an Iowa farm boy with his freshly minted doctorate from Johns Hopkins. At Hopkins, Day had come under the influence of Dr. E. V. McCollum, the father of scientific nutrition. "So I became interested in tooth decay and improper diet. When I started my graduate work in 1930, a fellow student was studying the nutritional significance of fluoride."

Day knew the stories about fluoride, how communities that had significant levels of fluoride in the drinking water seemed to have lower rates of cavities. "Well water is about one-tenth part per million fluoride; these communities had about ten parts per million," he remembers.

So when the chairman of the IU chemistry department asked if he would teach chemistry to beginning dental students, Day leaped at the chance.

Enter Joseph Muhler.

Muhler was an orphan who took a Greyhound from his hometown of Fort Wayne to Bloomington in 1942 and stuck around for three decades. The university treasurer at the time, Joseph A. Franklin, loaned him tuition money and got him a rent-free room with the chairman of the English department and a dishwashing job at the Sigma Kappa sorority house. Muhler was drafted in 1944, but in a strange but fateful turn of events, this caused him to be sent back to IU by the navy to study dentistry. In 1990, he recalled for a *Bloomington Herald-Times* reporter how he felt when he got his orders to go to dental school: "Oh God, no, I didn't even know what a tooth was. I probably hadn't even brushed my teeth."

And that's how he came to Harry Day's dental biochemistry class, as a reluctant dental student.

"Muhler sat in the front row," recalled Day. "Most of the students didn't give a hoot. They just wanted to fill teeth. But he got interested. I had told him when he wanted a project to work on, he could compare different fluorides but I'd be surprised if there was any difference."

The next year Muhler moved to the Indianapolis campus for his final year of dental school. "He needed income and the dental-health division of the state board of health offered him seventy-five dollars a month. He studied the effects of different fluorides. That was in 1946 and things started opening up. That's when he found stannous fluoride."

Crest didn't arrive fully formed on this planet. We can't pick one particular day as Crest's birthday; like any scientific achievement, Crest evolved over time, from classroom to laboratory to drugstore shelf. But one of the most significant dates in the development of Crest came in 1947. "The first definitive steps toward a general understanding of stannous fluoride and its possible usefulness in dental health came with a publication by Muhler and [Dr. Grant] Van Huysen [a professor of oral pathology at IU] in 1947. They reported that the compound had a marked effect on the acid-solubility of dental enamel," said Day.

The article, titled "Solubility of Enamel as Affected by Sodium Fluoride and Other Compounds" and published in the April 1947 issue of the *Journal of Dental Research,* was the first public report on the astonishing ability of stannous fluoride to prevent tooth decay. Buried among tables and prose was a statement that would change the habits of American families: "It is evident that a solution of sodium fluoride is a satisfactory agent to be used to reduce enamel solubility. The table shows, however, that other agents are just as good or better. A solution of stannous fluoride in this experiment has proved the most worthwhile agent to reduce solubility of powdered enamel."

This discovery, reported as it was in a small scholarly publication, would be little noted. But long remembered.

After receiving his dental degree in 1948, Muhler returned to Bloomington and started his graduate work in biochemistry under Day's direction. They chose rats for research subjects because rats' incisors grow continuously. No, they didn't brush the rats' teeth. "If you'd hold them, we'd brush them," jokes Day.

They fed the rats a diet designed to create cavities. "Corn would get lodged in their molars and set up areas of fermentation. We could produce experimental cavities that way." Soon the research was indicating that stannous fluoride would offer significant protection against cavities. So they knew that it worked on powdered dental enamel and on rat teeth. Would it work on humans? They needed a sponsor. Enter Procter & Gamble, the Cincinnati soap giant.

It was the IU connection that brought Procter & Gamble on board. "Joe and I attended the International Association for Dental Research in Evanston, Illinois, in 1949. He gave a paper and I sat in the audience," said Day. It turned out two IU chemistry grads, Verling Votaw and Arthur Radike, both employed in 1949 by P&G, were in attendance. "They sought us out that day. I knew them already." That started the ball rolling. P&G offered to fund the research.

In 1952 clinical tests were performed using 1,200 students in the Bloomington public schools. All were given plain white tubes of toothpaste, instructed in proper dental care and sent home with instructions to return in six months. The results of those tests were astonishing, every bit as miraculous as the "Look, Ma, no cavities!" ads would later portray them. Stannous fluoride reduced cavities by 83.1 percent!

The team got the patent—granted in 1955—and decided that half the royalties should go to the IU Foundation. In 1972, when the patent expired, the Crest royalties to Indiana University had reached $2.5 million.

Crest hit grocery and drugstore shelves in February 1955 and immediately grabbed a 12 percent market share. But there was no growth: 12 percent was it. Even the famous "Look, Ma, no cavities!" drawings by Norman Rockwell failed to nudge Crest's fortunes upward. That's when P&G went to work on the American Dental Association. For five years P&G worked to get the ADA to endorse Crest. It was an uphill battle. The group had never endorsed anything before. Not that Crest hadn't earned a recommendation. But the ADA was reluctant to endorse a commercial product, and with good reason: no professional organization of its stature had ever stuck its neck out for a commercial brand. In the end, the ADA chose the benefits over the risks. The group got nothing for the endorsement: no cash, no cases of toothpaste, just the feeling of a public served.

The legendary endorsement—"Crest has been shown to be an effective decay-preventive dentifrice when used in a conscientiously applied program of oral hygiene and regular professional care"—was published in the August 1, 1960, issue of the *Jour-*

nal of the American Dental Association. Soon those words would become familiar to television viewers everywhere. Crest sales doubled in a year, tripled in two years and in three years Crest was the number one-toothpaste in America.

Harry Day leads the walk into the chemistry building. It's a walk he makes five days a week. "I generally spend two to five hours a day here." He climbs the stairs to his second-floor office, a firm grip on the handrail his only concession to age. "I used to be on the fourth floor, ninety-six steps up."

Day has just finished an article on one of his role models, the late IU professor and administrator Herman Briscoe, for publication in *The Proceedings of the Indiana Academy of Science.*

But his major project is a comprehensive biography of E. V. McCollum, the father of scientific nutrition and his other role model. "I hope to have it done in another year and a half. Hope."

In the late-afternoon sun, Harry Day drives home to his cottage in a nearby retirement community. He'll have dinner, then head back home for some more work on the McCollum biography. Then off to bed. But not before one last task: "I brush with Crest. Every day."

In 1995, Crest was the most popular toothpaste in America by a long shot, with 31.6 percent of the toothpaste market, according to Information Resources, Inc. Colgate was second, with 19.5

percent. Mentadent, a relative newcomer, was third, with 9.9 percent. Fourth was Aqua-fresh, at 7.9 percent. Arm & Hammer rounded out the top five, with a 7.5 percent share of the market.

And that's a big market: in 1995 Americans purchased $1.5 billion worth of toothpaste.

Every one of the top brands now contains fluoride. But now they use sodium fluoride. Among dentists, stannous fluoride had come to be called "stain-us fluoride," because it mottled some people's teeth. Chemists found a way to use sodium fluoride and now it is an effective decay preventive dentifrice as well.

The hot thing in toothpastes now is "tartar control." In 1996 tartar control toothpastes accounted for 38.6 percent of sales. Second was "regular cavity fighting formula" (that would be fluoride) with 31.2 percent.

Other toothpaste sales by type:

Baking soda—12.5 percent
Baking soda and peroxide—8.0 percent
Tooth whitening—5.0 percent
Denture cleaner—1.3 percent
Denture cream—1.1 percent

My grandmother, who was born in the age of toothpaste, 1885, never used toothpaste. She didn't use a toothbrush either. She plucked a fresh twig each morning, frayed the end and dipped it in baking soda. Today the dentifrice industry is getting back to baking soda. When my grandmother died at seventy-five, she had all her teeth—which is more than lots of three-times-a-day folks can claim.

Flintstones Chewable Vitamins, Original—
60 Tablets—$4.98

The vitamin boom began in '96 . . . 1796. That was the year that
Scotsman James Lind convinced the British navy that limes
cured scurvy and that eating fresh vegetables prevented it.

A century later, Frederick Gowland Hopkins of Cambridge
University established the existence of vitamins. But it took an
American chemist with the unlikely name of Casimir Funk to
give them their name. He believed they were amines, which are
ammonium derivatives, and that they were vital, thus the name
vitamines. The "e" was later dropped so Dan Quayle could mis-
spell this word, too.

Today vitamins are a $4-billion-a-year business. One-fourth of
all vitamins are sold in drugstores. A medium-sized store can do
$21,000 a year in vitamins. Most vitamins are purchased in spe-
cialty vitamin stores and health stores: about half of the total sales.

The top-selling children's vitamins are Flintstones, with almost
30 percent of the market. How could this be? Who watches *The
Flintstones* anymore anyway? Plus, the movie version bombed,
even though it had John Goodman and Rosie O'Donnell. But kids
who didn't grow up watching Fred and Barney still prefer their vitamins. It must be something primitive. Bugs Bunny vitamins are
second on the kiddie-vitamin chart with a scant 6 percent of the market. And Garfield, who's in the paper every day, has only 3 percent.

Geritol—4-Ounce Tonic—$3.99

When I was growing up in the fifties, the three most feared diseases were cancer, stroke and iron-deficiency anemia ("tired

blood"). You still hear quite a bit about cancer and stroke, but when is the last time you heard anything about iron-deficiency anemia? Probably the last time you watched *Ted Mack's Original Amateur Hour,* and that went off the air in 1970.

I didn't know at the time, but Geritol was just a puppy, introduced to an unsuspecting public in 1950. Geritol, which was a combination of iron, sugar and alcohol, was a marketing phenomenon. In 1973, *Newsweek* called it "one of those rare consumer products that not only succeed, but that manage to etch themselves into the nation's consciousness in the process." Its commercials were so well known, they were the subject of comedy bits on every variety show. Even the phrase "the Geritol set" became a part of the language.

Ted Mack urged viewers to "Take Geritol. It builds iron power in your blood fast." A few years later, a healthy-looking actor would hug the healthy-looking actress at his side and tell the camera, "My wife, I think I'm going to keep her."

Geritol was as famous as Lucy's red hair.

There was only one problem. It didn't work, because most people who had "tired blood" weren't suffering from iron-deficiency anemia. They were working too much and sleeping too little. The Federal Trade Commission began investigating Geritol's claims in 1959. Eight years later—the FTC must have suffered from tired blood, too—the commission ordered the tired-blood commercials off the air. Geritol didn't do that, but it did reformulate its product to include seven more essential vitamins. The commercials continued to run, so the FTC went to court. And in 1973, a mere fourteen years after the whole thing started, a New York federal court judge ruled that Geritol's ads were deceptive, bordering on "recklessness." He agreed with the FTC that the Geritol ads didn't make clear to the viewing audience that the vast majority of tired people weren't suffering from iron-deficiency anemia. The judge fined Geritol's manufacturer $812,000, which was then a record fine (since eclipsed by the O.J. case and scores of shop teachers who lost their fingers to saw blades).

It had taken the FTC only fourteen years to crack down on Geritol. That was two years less than it took the agency to get Carter Products to stop advertising that Carter's Little Liver Pills could beat lethargy and the blues.

Geritol is still on drugstore shelves, still pitching its iron and vitamin tonic (12 percent alcohol) as a panacea for tired blood and that rundown feeling. It's just that not nearly as many people believe anymore.

Polident Powder—3-Ounce Can—$2.35

There are no photographs of George Washington—he predated George Eastman and Edwin Land by a century or so—but we know what he looked like from the dollar bill. He was a striking fellow, with a receding hairline, pretty gray locks, a bulbous nose and full cheeks. All those details come from the most famous portrait of the first president, the one that Gilbert Stuart painted in 1796 and was later used as a model for George's dollar bill portrait and his Mount Rushmore statuary.

What isn't so well known is that those full cheeks belonged not to George, but to a couple of balls of cotton wadding that Stuart insisted the president put in his mouth, to fill out his face and rid him of his sunken cheeks. That sucked-in look came from the fact that Washington was virtually toothless. No, he wasn't from eastern Kentucky. He was from the dark ages of dentistry, when every dental malady was remedied by the same cure: pull it. Washington lost his first tooth at twenty-two—it hurt, so the dentist jerked it out. He had only a handful—not a mouthful—of teeth at the time of the Stuart sitting. And at age sixty-three his final molar was removed.

Washington had a set of false teeth—two sets, in fact—but they weren't satisfactory for even a moment of repose, much less a meal. One set had been crafted by one Paul Revere, the same fellow who had had such success shouting "The British are coming! The British are coming!" Revere was a great messenger. And a great patriot. But Revere was a silversmith by trade; Washington's teeth were carved of ivory. Give Revere his due, however, the other set, by a tradesman, was no better.

If only there had been Polident and its companion product, Poly-grip, the denture holding cream, in George's day, his dentures might have set better in his mouth. For sure they would have been sparkling clean: Polident is powdered toothpaste. If you could take out your real teeth and soak them in toothpaste, it would be a more efficient way to clean them, too.

Nyquil—10-Ounce Bottle—$9.99

I live in Kentucky, where the preachers and the bootleggers join forces every four years or so to campaign against legalizing liquor. Some urban areas are "wet," meaning we have such civilized modern conveniences as drive-through liquor stores. Meanwhile, out in the sticks, we have "dry" counties, where the sale of alcoholic beverages is forbidden. It can lead to strange combinations. For instance, in Kentucky, Bourbon County is dry, while Christian County is wet.

A pharmacist friend tells me that years ago in the dry counties, NyQuil was the best-selling product in the drugstore.
Why? Because years ago it was 40 percent alcohol. Today it's
only, oh, 17 percent alcohol. Procter & Gamble reformulated
the product in 1993, dropping the alcohol content from 25 percent. The company was reacting to guidelines set forth by the
Non-Prescription Drug Association (of which P&G is a member and a driving force behind the guidelines) and also reacting to the marketplace. NyQuil sales had been slipping as the
public turned away from drugs with heavy alcohol concentra-
tions.

Captopril—100 Tablets—$5

The generic drug industry was born of military cost cutting.
Hard to believe when you consider the notorious thousand-
dollar toilet seats and five-hundred-dollar hammers that the
army has purchased over the years.

But generic drugs came to be in a couple of shoe boxes on a
filing cabinet in an FDA office. In the early forties, the agency
used the file cards to decide which generics could be purchased
by the armed forces. We were in a war at the time, and cost cutting was an important part of the war effort. Since generics were
cheaper and essentially the same as name brands, the FDA kept
this little filing system for the military.

When the war ended, a movement started to allow civilians to
purchase generics too. Pharmacists were among the earliest sup-
porters of generics. As might be expected, big drug companies
were not. The pharmaceutical giants fought against generics and
in the fifties their lobbyists managed to get antisubstitution laws

passed in every state—even Alaska and Hawaii, and they were barely states. Then came Naderism, the consumer activist movement that began when Ralph Nader bought a Corvair and found that it was unsafe at any speed. When Nader's followers turned their attention to the drug industry, they began to ask questions about generics, like why shouldn't consumers pay less for the same drug without all the fancy television commercials? Between 1979 and 1983, antisubstitution laws were repealed in all fifty states.

It was the federal government that really got the generic industry going with the passage in 1984 of the Wasman-Hatch Act (unlike a previous Hatch act, it has nothing to do with teenage girls or state borders). Essentially, it gave the big drug companies their due, extending the patent life of a drug and granting a company a period of market exclusivity, while giving the generic industry its due as well. Generic companies can now begin developing a generic version of a patented drug while it is still under patent, making it possible for the generic company to begin marketing the generic as soon as the patent expires.

In 1980, when the generic war was being waged in state legislatures, only 2 percent of prescriptions were filled with generic drugs. Today, 45 percent of all prescriptions are filled with generics. And predictions are this will rise to 65 percent by the turn of the century.

Do generics save money? Does your druggist work on an elevated platform? When Bristol-Myers Squibb's patent on the blood-pressure medicine Capoten expired on February 13, 1996, the price for one hundred tablets of it was fifty-six dollars. The next day, you could buy a comparably sized bottle of the generic captopril for five dollars. It's called competition. Suddenly twelve companies were selling the drug instead of one.

Rogaine Update, Two Months Later

I'm feeling the pressure.

Not the pressure of 50,000 new hair follicles pressing down on my pate. That's not happening. I'm feeling the pressure of eyes staring at my head. Of voices asking me every day, "Well, is it working?"

And I answer them all the same: "Something is happening."

Something IS happening on the top of my head.

Little hairs are springing up and turning into big long hairs.

Not a great number of little hairs. In fact, I could probably count them. But they are springing up and that's something that hasn't happened on my forehead since Nixon was president.

It is now Day 60 of my Great Rogaine Experiment.

The box doesn't promise miracles, which is good because I'm not seeing miracles. People are not running up to me on the street asking to rub that lush crop of new hair.

No, people are just staring. And asking that familiar question, "Well, is it working?"

It is working.

At the halfway point of my experiment I can say without equivocation that I have new hair growth.

How much new hair growth? For now, let's just

say hair is growing but I haven't been out comb shopping just yet.

So this time it's the Bald Vince Effect. People remember me as balder than I am. So when they see me again—especially if they know about my Great Rogaine Experiment—they think I am growing hair.

I am and I'm not. But the box says to give it four months.

So let's give it four months.

What Rogaine Is Like

I always assumed Rogaine was a gel that you rubbed into your scalp. It's actually a thin liquid that you spray on the bald areas.

It doesn't sting. The first time I sprayed it on I thought I felt a tingle, but I've felt nothing since. It smells, but not bad. Sort of like hair spray, or at least what I remember hair spray smelling like from my hirsute youth.

My mother worries that I will get the spray in my eyes. I asked her why, was she afraid I'd grow hair in my eyes?

It's painless. The only pain is trying to remember that I have to spray it on twice a day, every morning and every night. And the pain of spending thirty dollars a month.

7

From the Underarm
to the Top of the Shorts:
The Real Middle America

For an area of the body that doesn't get much exposure—or respect—the underarm sure gets the money.

Secret Roll-On, Original Scent—2.7 Ounces—$2.98

Fun fact: 98 percent of American men and women use deodorant.

Scary, not-so-fun fact: 2 percent don't.

And I always seem to get in line behind a member of that 2 percent.

It's not a question of whether or not we as a people stink, but whether we as a people *think* we stink. And the answer is a resounding $1.4 billion *yes*.

That's how much Americans spent in 1996 on deodorants: $1.4 billion. It's an enormous number—and an enormous market. But not necessarily a growth market. Most of us use deodorant already. So sales increases in this market pretty much mirror the population growth. Brands are just fighting each other for market share.

And the winner of this fight, no sweat, is Secret. Secret is America's favorite deodorant, with 12.9 percent of the deodorant market. That translates to $185 million in annual sales.

Secret is, of course, a women's deodorant. Which brings us to the number-two deodorant in America: Right Guard. A man's deodorant. Right Guard has 9.6 percent of the market. Rounding out the top five are Arrid, with an 8.4 percent share, Sure, with 7.8 percent, and Ban, with 7.7 percent.

We first noticed that we smelled bad back in the days when we lived five families to a cave. Actually, we weren't the first to notice. The animals were, according to renowned anthropologist Louis Leakey. Dr. Leakey speculated that early man was able to survive because of his body odor. He believed that early man smelled so bad that other animals couldn't stand to be around us—sort of like an engineer at a supermodels convention—much less eat us. This distinctive b.o. was so disgusting that it turned the stomachs of predatory animals who otherwise would have had us for lunch. Literally. Leakey came up with this rather unusual thesis after watching wild baboons and chimpanzees. Young baboons are often eaten by predators, but chimpanzees—our closest relatives—aren't. This is because predators find their smell disgusting.

Body odor is just the smell of sweat. And sweat is part of the body's thermostat system. When we get too hot, the sweat glands release moisture to cool the skin. Antiperspirants try to counter this natural system, working to prevent the release of sweat. Deodorants work to mask the odor. At one time, deodorants and antiperspirants were two separate categories—some folks preferred deodorizing their sweat, others didn't want to sweat at all. Now most products in this category are both: deodorant and antiperspirant.

Before commercial deodorants, women used a solution of ammonia and water to scrub their underarms. The first commercial deodorant—actually an antiperspirant—was Mum, which hit the market in 1888. It used zinc oxide as its active ingredient. And while it did a good job of halting perspiration, it also did a good job of disinfecting stables and slaughterhouses, of refining crude oil, and of irritating human skin and staining cotton clothing.

At the turn of the century, Mum was surpassed by Everdry Anti-Perspirant, a thin liquid that stung the crap out of your underarm, which ladies of the day took to mean it was effective. But it too stained clothing.

In the thirties came liquid nonperspirants, which took fifteen minutes to set up but effectively closed down the sweat glands for days. Then during the forties researchers discovered that aluminum chlorohydrate had the same antiperspirant properties as zinc oxide but without the problems, so it is now the active ingredient in many deodorants.

Ban—4-Ounce Bottle—$3.29

Mum, the original deodorant, was a cream and so were many popular deodorants over the years. In the forties, sprays ruled. In the fifties, Bristol-Myers was looking for a new way to apply deodorant. Creams and lotions were messy. Sprays went everywhere. How about a roll-on? You'd never have to touch the deodorant. So in 1951 the company introduced Mum Rollette, which used the same technology as the ballpoint pen. The problem was that the deodorant lotion inside this new kind of applicator ate the plastic ball. Once women saw that, they defected from Mum in droves: it eats the plastic ball, wonder what it does to my underarm? Back to the lab. Four hundred eighty tries later, Bristol-Myers had a plastic ball that didn't gum up and didn't deteriorate; in short, it actually worked.

Mum Rollette had a bad image, so Bristol-Myers created a new name: Ban—as in Ban b.o. Ban hit drugstore shelves in February 1955, and by year's end it was number three with a bullet. Two years later it was number one.

Mennen Speed Stick—$2.19

Any fan of the corner drugstore should buy Mennen products because the company's founder, Gerhard Mennen, owned the old corner drugstore in Newark, New Jersey. It was there that he developed his first drugstore hit, Mennen's Sure Corn Killer, in 1878. Mennen's Speed Stick, the company's most successful product, was the first stick deodorant when it arrived in stores in 1958. Today, the most popular type of deodorant is the solid or stick: 60.1 percent of deodorants sold in 1995. Sprays comprised 17.7 percent and roll-ons 14.8 percent. Creams, the original antiperspirant medium, ranked fourth, a distant fourth, with 7.4 percent.

Lee Press-On Nails, Extra Long—$1.78

Has there been a more useless invention in the history of mankind than the acrylic fingernail? (Okay, maybe the Chia

Pet.) Long fingernails are in and of themselves worthless. But to invent an artificial long fingernail? It's the height of foolishness. (Okay, maybe *Ace Ventura: When Nature Calls* was the height of foolishness—but this is close.)

This fixation with fingernails goes back a long way. In ancient Egypt, the upper classes took to staining their nails a rich clay color, using coloring from a shrub leaf. At about the same time over in China, the aristocracy painted the nails with a mixture of beeswax, egg whites, gelatin and gum Arabic.

Long nails have always been a sign of indolence—"Look at me, I don't do heavy lifting for a living, I don't work with my hands"—and therefore wealth. And by extension, a sign of good taste. In the seventeenth century it was considered bad form to knock on someone's door. The polite thing to do was to scratch. The longer the nails, the louder the scratch. Poor working-class folks must have stood outside in the rain for hours waiting for the folks inside to hear their nailless scratching.

In the seventeenth century, the Chinese were coloring their fingernails by injecting dye into them. The dyes were injected under the cuticle and the nail would grow out precolored. Pretty, but *ouch!*

The father of the modern manicure—that's right; father, not mother—was King Louis Philippe's foot doctor, Monsieur Sitts. After removing a royal hangnail, he got the idea to create a manicure system (sounds like an infomercial product: Dr. Sitts's Manicure System, just $29.95). He adapted an orange-wood stick from the dental trade and began giving manicures around the kingdom, and not a moment too soon to suit the leisure class's tastes. You see, before Sitts, manicures were extremely painful—the tools of the trade were scissors and acid. Yikes!

When Sitts died, he willed his nail trade to his niece, who continued working for France's royal family. In 1892 she advertised herself as an "artiste of the hand."

The Sitts's manicure system was carried over to this country, and by the end of the nineteenth century, there were manicure parlors all over. Riker's Manicure Parlour in Manhattan took up several floors of a building, with each floor indulging women of different incomes. In 1903, a writer compared the number of nail shops to the number of saloons and found them about the same. It wasn't until the twenties that beauty salons introduced hairstylists, in the process dropping manicurists a notch in stature.

In the early part of this century, "nail rouge"—as nail coloring was called—was considered vulgar. These colorings were made by soaking alkanet root in alcohol. The first commercial nail product was introduced in 1917 by Cutex. It was a buff that gave nails a gloss. In 1925, Cutex introduced a liquid called "nail lacquer," a rosy pink coloring that was dabbed on the center of the nail. That was the fashion—and would be until the father of nail polish arrived on the scene.

The father of fingernail polish was Charles Revson, who teamed with a chemist named Charles Lachman in 1932 to create a nail polish made from color pigments rather than dyes. Now real nail colors were possible. More than anything, Revson was a marketing genius. He gave his nail polish colors names. The practice at the time was to sell by numbers. And he also sold women on the idea of matching their nail color to their lipstick shade. His company, Revlon, is still a leader in the cosmetic industry. The name is a combination of Revson and Lachman. Well, if you squint, it's a combination of Revson and Lachman.

The precursor to Lee Press-On Nails were porcelains, long fake nails made popular in the early seventies by such celebrities as Diana Ross and Cher. A thin, brittle acrylic nail was introduced in the seventies, but it wasn't until the eighties that fake nails could pass for real.

Fingernails have a lot in common with hair—neither has any living cells, both grow continuously but slowly. Nails grow about an eighth of an inch a week.

If you are right-handed, the nails on your right hand will grow faster than the nails on your left hand. And if you are a typist or pianist or in some other profession that involves using your fingers a lot, your fingernails will grow faster than average. Also, middle fingers grow faster, a fact that should provide endless mirth among junior high school–age readers of this book. If it seems like you are cutting your nails more often in the summer, there's a reason for that: you are cutting your nails more often in the summer. Nails grow faster in warm weather. They also grow faster during the day, during pregnancy and just before a period. Men's nails grow faster than women's. And fingernails grow about four times faster than toenails.

Women spend $170 million a year on artificial nails and $260 million a year on fingernail polish, some of it white in color, which brings things full circle, because the fingernail is actually white, but the blood vessels in the nail bed make them look pink.

Band-Aids—30-Count Assorted—$1.99

People get a total of 35 million wounds a year in this country, according to a survey by 3M Health Care. What a fun survey that must have been to work on: "Any wounds in your household the past twelve months? Lots of blood?" Of those 35 million cuts, scrapes and abrasions, half are left to heal uncovered, even though studies have proven that is the wrong thing to do. Sorry, Mom. (My mom always said air helped heal a cut, but scientific studies show that moist wounds heal faster than dry wounds.)

And what do most of us cover our wounds with? Band-Aids!

Americans spent $412.3 million on first aid in 1996, and drugstores got almost half of that. First aid covers a number of different items, from Band-Aids (adhesive bandages is the correct term) to gauze and cotton.

And when Americans think first aid, they think Johnson & Johnson, the Band-Aid people. J&J is number one in sales of first-aid items.

Band-Aids, like chocolate bunnies, are a seasonal item. Unlike chocolate bunnies, their season isn't limited to Easter, but it is a narrow season. Band-Aid sales start heading upward in May, peak in June and bottom out from November to April. Common sense will tell you why: kids are out of school, running around the countryside, banging into trees and swings, hitting each other with balls and bats, starting knife fights. Actually, knife fights are a year-round activity. But summer means more than sun—it also means scrapes and cuts.

The Band-Aid of today is pretty much the same as the Band-Aid of my youth (the fifties and sixties) and the Band-Aid of my mother's youth (the thirties).

There is one difference of note: they no longer put that goofy little tear string on the Band-Aid package. That useless orange twine was supposed to help you open the pack, which was sealed to keep the bandage sterile. Johnson & Johnson gave in to popular practices in 1992, as much as admitting that nobody used the string. When you need a Band-Aid, you need it in a hurry. So you rip off the paper wrapper. But dropping that string was a big deal, duly noted in *The New York Times*. After all, that little string had been in the Band-Aid wrapper for seventy years.

It was a pharmacist who saw the need for a Band-Aid–like bandage. Robert Johnson, who owned a drugstore in Brooklyn, heard an address by the British surgeon Sir Joseph Lister, who believed wound infections came from germs. What? Germs! An unheard of concept in 1876, when Lister spoke to the Philadelphia Medical Congress. Most physicians of the time treated wounds with a sawdust compress—sawdust! And not sterile sawdust, but the common sweepings from a sawmill. Considering the state of nineteenth-century medicine, it's amazing as many of our ancestors made it to the twentieth century as did.

Lister spoke of the need for sterile, germ-free dressings, and Robert Johnson believed. He gathered up his brothers James, an engineer, and Edward, a lawyer, to form Johnson & Johnson— we don't know why the company name was one Johnson short. They sold prepackaged bandages that were an immediate hit among army field surgeons.

Not content to rest on their Johnsons, they soon introduced Johnson's Baby Powder. But the brothers' greatest contribution to American culture—and American drugstores' bottom line— was a tiny wound cover that was actually invented in 1920 by a cotton buyer in the company's purchasing department. When the wife of Earle Johnson (no relation) burned herself cooking, Earle first reached for one of the company's surgical dressings. But it was too large. So he improvised, covering the burn with gauze and holding it in place with adhesive tape. As his wife kept burning herself, he kept making up these little bandages. Finally he got an idea—make the bandages in quantity. He whipped up a few, using crinoline fabric to cover the sticky part of the adhesive. When he showed his invention to company president James Johnson (not the Johnson who married his nurse and left her the family fortune—that was a later Johnson), Johnson was impressed by Johnson's invention. And thus was born the Band-Aid.

All except for the name, which was suggested by the plant superintendent at the company's New Brunswick, New Jersey, facility, one W. Johnson Kenyon. Are you noticing this Johnson pattern?

It was, of course, not an immediate hit.

The Band-Aid's success can be traced to the efforts of the company's research chief, Dr. Frederick Kilmer. Kilmer had a writing gene in him—his son was the tree poet Joyce Kilmer—and he began inundating the American media with articles about this new medical marvel. (Please, let's not even think about what might have happened had he enlisted his son in the campaign: "I think that I have never made/A poem as useful as a Band-Aid . . .")

Brilliant marketing strategy number two came in 1924 when the company gave free Band-Aids to every Boy Scout troop in America. Who do you think is responsible for many of those 35 million wounds a year? Little boys playing in the woods with knives, maybe? It's been a staple in first-aid kits ever since.

Ben-Gay Original—2-Ounce Tube—$5.09

Ben-Gay is not the name of the lead character in a Fire Island
revue. It's the name of the most famous sore-muscle ointment
of all time, a balm that penetrates to give the user relief from
pain, flexibility in the joints and the smell of an old people's
home.

Its name comes from its inventor, the French pharmacist Jules
Bengue. But the French, with their notorious disdain for all
things American, were sure no one in the United States could
properly pronounce Bengue. It would come out "Ben-gwee" or
"Ben-guu." So when the salve was first imported in 1898, the
name was spelled phonetically. Voilà—Ben-Gay.

Hey, isn't voilà French? We seem to be able to pronounce that.

Compound W—2-Ounce Tube—$3.49

Americans bought $45.2 million worth of wart removers in
1996. They could have saved a lot of money by calling my father. He could take a wart off in a fingersnap. He had a secret
ceremony he'd perform, so secret that I never saw him do it. My
mother says he'd steal a dishrag, rub it on the wart, then bury it
in the backyard. I swear it took a wart off me.

For those whose fathers aren't quite so handy, there's Compound W, Wart Off and the new Occlusal-HP, which *Drug Topics* calls the "least promoted prescription to over-the-counter
switch of all time." Frankly, it's hard to get the public excited
about a wart remover.

All commercial wart removers contain 17 percent salicylic

acid. That means they remove your wart by eating it off. So don't put wart remover on anything besides a wart.

Or a dishrag.

Cutex Fingernail Polish Remover— 2-Ounce Bottle—$1.09

Fingernail polish remover is sort of like duct tape for women. Women use it to remove virtually everything. And it works. You can remove stains and extra glue, even fingernail polish. So here's the question of the day: If fingernail polish remover removes everything, what removes fingernail polish remover?

I really needed to know recently.

The interior rearview mirror in my car fell off and I put it back on with Super Glue. I am, as far as I know, the first person in America who has been able to pull off that feat. When I tell others about it, they always say, "Yeah, my rearview mirror fell off once, too, but I couldn't get Super Glue to work." Not only did I get it to work, I got it to work three times. My rearview mirror falls off about once a year and each time I put it back on with Super Glue. But the last time, the little metal button wouldn't come out of the mirror. (I glue the button on, then slide the mirror onto the button.) I don't have the strength—or the patience—to hold the entire mirror while the glue sets. So I had to get the button un–Super Glued from the mirror.

What to do? Fingernail polish remover, my son the auto mechanic said. So I soaked the mirror in fingernail polish overnight. When that didn't work I tried it for a second night, thinking maybe that because so much of the fingernail polish remover had evaporated the first night that it would take two overnights. That didn't work either. What it did do was leave a crust of fingernail polish remover in what had been a perfectly serviceable cat food bowl. So the question now became: What removes fingernail polish remover?

The answer: dishwashing detergent. We soaked that sucker in dishwashing detergent and it came right off.

And I went out and bought a new rearview mirror.

Fingernail polish remover is primarily acetone, a solvent that's good on all sorts of things including oil, rubber, plastic, lacquer and varnish, which explains why it's so good at removing fingernail polish and lots of other things. It's a by-product in the manufacture of butyl alcohol—it's alcohol, in other words—which explains why it evaporates so quickly.

Vaseline Petroleum Jelly—3.75-Ounce Jar—$2.59

Vaseline is the WD-40 of the drugstore. Whatever your problem, Vaseline can fix it. It promotes the healing of cuts, it keeps the pocket of your baseball glove flexible, it removes stains from the sofa, and if you and the little woman are having one of those "lubrication" problems, just reach for the Vaseline.

Unlike many drugstore items, Vaseline wasn't invented. It was discovered, literally, in a Pennsylvania oil well, where the stiff, sticky stuff oozed up, seizing up the drilling rigs—like cholesterol in an old man's veins—and making life miserable for the workers, who hated the stuff.

But one Robert Chesebrough—whose name would later be

immortalized as the first half of the Chesebrough-Ponds cosmetics company—saw opportunity where oil men saw oozing gook.

Chesebrough, a Brooklyn kerosene salesman, had ventured west to Titusville, Pennsylvania, in 1859, when oil riggers had gone on strike, effectively putting him out of work. That's when he saw them struggling with this petroleum jelly stuff. The only time the riggers didn't hate it was when they cut themselves trying to free up the equipment it had frozen. Then—they had discovered—a dab of the stuff helped the cut heal faster.

So Chesebrough lugged a bucket of the stuff back to Brooklyn, where he tinkered with it in his home lab. He managed to extract the petroleum jelly from the sludge and began experimenting. On himself. He would cut himself and rub on the jelly. Then he would burn himself and rub on the jelly. The jellied cuts and burns seemed to heal faster than the others. Did I mention that when he experimented on himself, he would make two cuts, one for the jelly and the other as a control?

Instead of Chesebrough's Magic Jelly, he called it Vaseline, because he stored it in his wife's vases and because other magic potions of the day ended in "ine" (Listerine, to name one).

It soon became the Vaseline All-Purpose Petroleum Jelly. Folks were using it for all sorts of things, from protecting baby's butt to removing tiny hands from tiny cookie jars to oiling squeaky doors. Druggists liked it because it made a nice base for their own medicinal concoctions. Chesebrough himself preferred it with a glass of milk. That's right: he ate the stuff and tried to convince the world to eat a heaping spoonful a day. Thank God they didn't have television commercials back then.

But then again, Chesebrough lived to be ninety-six, and no one ever heard him squeak.

8
The Stomach: Clearinghouse for the Soul, Repository for the Burger

Don't think that the only connection between the drugstore and the stomach is Pepto-Bismol. You can also fill your stomach there.

Soda Fountain Hamburger and Coke—$3.05

At Wagner's Pharmacy, the soda fountain is right up front as you enter the door. If it seems like that's the tail wagging the dog, it is, except in this case, it's the horse. Wagner's is located on the corner of Fourth Street and Central Avenue in Louisville, Kentucky, catty-corner from Churchill Downs.

It's where horse trainers eat breakfast, where millionaire horse owners rub shoulders with down-on-their-luck bookies. Jockeys eat here, as do their agents. But so too do regular folks from the neighborhood.

Wagner's just happens to be in an unusual neighborhood.

Still, it's an old-fashioned soda fountain and it's old-fashioned soda fountain talk you hear. Waitresses tell people they've never met all their problems. Folks borrow salt shakers without asking, or needing to, just a smile and a nod.

Wagner's is a throwback to that time when the drugstore was a community center. Unlike the hardware store or the grocery, the beauty parlor or the barbershop, drugstores truly were a meeting place for the town. Hardware stores were—and still are—guy places. Groceries were where women congregated. Barbershops and beauty parlors, until recent times, weren't unisex. But everyone met at the drugstore.

How was it that the drugstore came to be the town hall for every small town in America? There are lots of reasons—everyone comes to the drugstore at some time, and there's always that waiting period while the pharmacist prepares the prescription.

But one thing set drugstores apart from other retail establishments, one thing made them appealing to folks looking to gather and talk: the soda fountain. Soda fountains weren't just for lunch. They were for breakfast and midmorning coffee, they were for afternoon smokes and after-school Cokes. The arrangement—everyone sitting around one long bar—made for easy communication. That bar was the great equalizer. Judges sat next to lawyers, not looked down at them. Bosses and secretaries ate side by side.

According to an October 1933 article in *American Druggist,* the first soda fountain in this country was in Elias Durand's Philadelphia apothecary. The French-born Durand had imported an apparatus for making and vending carbonic-acid water, and he opened this primitive soda fountain—have your ever tasted carbonic-acid water? Do you want to?—in 1825.

He opened it at the right time. Soda water, with its crisp taste, was becoming a national obsession, a way for even teetotalers to get a rush from their drink.

The Franklin Institute's centennial celebration in 1874 was

the scene of the soda fountain's great leap forward. One Robert Green, who had the soda water concession, ran out of sweet cream, a favorite soda water additive of the day. He hustled around, and the closest substitute he could find was ice cream. And thus was born the ice cream soda. (This is the generally accepted story for the invention of the ice cream soda. There are others.)

Soda fountains started springing up in the 1890s, as the dry forces took on the saloons and liquor stores. And the soda fountain literally boomed in 1919 with the passage of the Volstead Act, which mandated national prohibition.

Soda fountains and drugstores were a natural fit because pharmacists knew syrups and carbonation. The Federal Census of Distribution for 1919 counted 54,745 independent drugstores, 31,813 of them with soda fountains. That's 60 percent. And of the 3,513 chain drugstores, 3,031 had soda fountains. That's even higher: 84 percent. In 1935, soda fountains sold $121 million worth of meals: almost 7 percent of the total eat-out tab for the country.

But if one event can be said to have brought the soda fountain to the masses, it was the invention in 1886 of Coca-Cola. Coke was invented, of course, by a pharmacist, Atlanta druggist John S. Pemberton.

A few years later, C. D. Bradham invented a similar soda water concoction, which he called Brad's Drink, at the pharmacy in New Bern, North Carolina. Of course, as the line went, his drink was aimed at those who think young. He later changed the name to Pepsi—because of the drink's ability to cure dyspepsia (indigestion)—and it too became a soda fountain staple.

In 1948, 60 percent of drugstores had soda fountains, according to that year's edition of *Remington's Practice of Pharmacy*.

"The basis of soda fountain service is the flavoring syrups which are used as vehicles in prescriptions. Carbonated beverages have their medicinal uses as well as their uses for refreshments. . . . The widespread sale of other confections in drugstores is therefore understandable."

A number of famous people got their introduction to the workaday world at a drugstore soda fountain. Harry S. Truman, who would go on to run a haberdasher store—and then become vice president under Franklin Roosevelt, and president when Roosevelt died—worked at Clinton's Drug Store in Independence, Missouri. Bob Dole, who was only 10 or so percentage points from the presidency in 1996, worked at a soda fountain in Russell, Kansas. Lucille Ball, James Garner and many others who didn't go on to become movie stars learned to turn fizz and swizzle and squirt into a refreshing drink behind the counter at the local drugstore soda fountain.

The soda fountain reigned supreme into the sixties. By 1965, though, soda fountains were still a teen hangout, but no longer *the* teen hangout. Drive-in restaurants—we had one called Trayer's—had supplanted soda fountains among teens. The food was the same, greasy and fast. But closing time was later; you could hang out at the drive-in well past sunset.

And up the road from Armour loomed a new challenger, a shiny, stainless-steel hamburger emporium with walk-up service and a parking lot where they never hustled you home. We already had a McDonald's in 1965. And it would be McDonald's that killed the soda fountains of town—my town, your town, every town.

Not that McDonald's set out to kill the soda fountain. Or

change the face of every town in America. Wal-Mart didn't set out to destroy downtown businesses either, but the effects were the same.

Times were changing anyway. Could the drugstore have been the hangout of the seventies? The seventies were the age of drugs—illicit ones—and it's hard to imagine shaggy-headed teens trying to sneak a hit of weed in plain view of a trained drug specialist, a man sworn to uphold the integrity and honor of the drug trade. The day of the drugstore as a gathering place for folks of all ages was past.

There are still soda fountains in America. They are not dinosaurs. Dinosaurs are extinct. Soda fountains still exist. You just have to go a ways to find them.

Where I live, in Louisville, Kentucky, I'm within easy driving distance of three drugstores with soda fountains: Wagner's Pharmacy near the track, Zeiden's Third Avenue Pharmacy downtown and the Charlestown Rexall just across the Ohio river in Charlestown, Indiana. Three soda fountains for a town of one million isn't much. But it's better than none.

For a chocolate malted the way Dottie used to make down at the Corner Drug, try this recipe:

1½ tablespoons malted milk powder
1 tablespoon chocolate syrup
½ cup milk (cold, of course)
3 scoops chocolate ice cream

Mix all ingredients in a blender at low speed for 30 seconds, or until smooth. Gulp it down as if it were your last drink.

For a list of Corner Drug stores with soda fountains, see the appendix.

Slim-Fast—12-Ounce Can—$1.25

It's called the liquid meal-replacement category, and next to stool softener, it's the least appetizing-sounding category in the old Corner Drug. Unfortunately, it's supposed to be appetizing. Or at least filling. What it really is is a milk shake in a can.

The Slim-Fast story begins in 1945 when veteran Daniel Abraham purchased the San-Cura Itch-Relief Ointment company—not a likely beginning for a diet drink. But the husky Abraham was always interested in diet products. He brought out his first one, Slim-Mint gum, in 1956. It was a chewing gum with benzocaine in it to dull your hunger—and your tongue. It bombed. In 1960 he tried again, this time with the diet pill Figure-Aid. No success. Abraham finally hit big in 1976 with Dexatrim, yet another diet pill, this one an appetite suppressant with phenylpropanolamine in it.

But his biggest success wouldn't arrive until the next year. Slim-Fast was initially a powdered drink mix, and it took a while to take off—slowed in part by the deaths of dieters using a different product. But when talk-show diva Oprah Winfrey lost a highly publicized sixty-seven pounds—the equivalent of four bowling balls—while using the liquid meal replacement Opti-fast, all America took notice. And when they found out Optifast cost $6,000 a year, they took notice of the inexpensive Slim-Fast. The company quickly capitalized on the liquid meal-replacement fad by signing up porky baseball manager Tommy

Lasorda as its spokesman. Many Americans have since moved on to prescription diet drugs, but for those looking for a liquid meal replacement, Slim-Fast is still the lunch of champions, with an 88 percent market share.

Castor Oil—4-Ounce Bottle—$1.59

"Nearly all men die of their remedies and not of their illnesses."

—Molière, *Le malade imaginaire*

Anyone who has ever taken castor oil will agree with the French farcist on that one. Castor oil, which in my youth was considered the cure for just about everything, is a laxative, nothing more, nothing less. It's still found in most medicine cabinets, it's just shoved to the back. Nineties moms no longer reach for a laxative at the first sign of distress. Now they reach for the children's Tylenol or the phone to call the doctor.

Castor oil belongs in that group of products that June Cleaver used but are now out of style. Others in the category include Carter's Little Liver Pills—now known simply as Carter's Little Pills—Geritol, Doan's Pills and even Contac, the miracle cold pill of the sixties and seventies. They have all been lapped by more modern miracle drugs. We no longer trust drugs made from common roots and shrubs. We want miracle drugs synthesized by white-coated scientists in some faraway lab. We want science!

But, once, every malady had its own home remedy. And each neighborhood had its healer, a sort of midwife of childhood. In my neighborhood it was the lady next door, whom everyone called Mammy. A bee sting? Let me rub three different grasses on it. Sore throat? Sleep with a sock filled with Vicks VapoRub around your neck. The crazy thing is that all these remedies worked.

But with the coming of science, many of these cures have fallen by the wayside, perhaps simply fallen out of favor. Each onetime remedy has its own tale of woe. It happens in every industry—ask the guys who used to make plumed hats.

But in the drug industry, the cycles are sometimes accelerated by outside forces, in particular the federal government. In the case of over-the-counter remedies, that has been the case in the last quarter-century, since the Food and Drug Administration was forced off its constipated seat by the Food, Drug and Cosmetics Act of 1962, which decreed that all drugs, new or old, had to be safe and effective. Before 1962, the operative word was "safe." Therefore, drug companies could invent illnesses and then market drugs to cure them—I'm thinking in particular here of Geritol and "tired blood."

So Carter's Little Liver Pills could fight lethargy. Carter's Little Pills now contain bisacodyl, a mild laxative, which will certainly affect a part of your body near your liver.

But of all these old-timey medicines, none was more old-timey than castor oil. Just the mention of the words *castor oil* could send a kid running for cover. Castor oil tastes exactly like what it's supposed to purge from your body. It's one of the oldest medicines in the drugstore, dating to ancient Egypt. Hippocrates knew—and wrote—of its powers. A medical encyclopedia from 1866 recommends it as a treatment for pneumonia.

India is the world's top castor oil producer, making 950,000 tons a year. Castor oil is extracted from the seed of the ricinus bean (sometimes called the castor bean). The hulls are removed and the seed is pressed. This first pressing yields medicinal castor oil. A second pressing produces a lubricant used in machinery and brake fluid and as a dressing for baseball gloves and other leather goods. The remaining residue can be used as fertilizer.

But don't try this at home. The bean also contains ricin, a poison.

Castor oil is also used in fly paper, in hard candy and in embalming fluid. Most lipstick is 20 percent castor oil. Ugh. Most of us are just as happy it has fallen out of favor as a medicine. Castor oil was truly a case of the cure being worse than the disease.

Tagamet HB 200—16 Tablets—$5.89

If you had arrived on this planet in the fall of 1995 and were trying to decipher this unique American culture, you might have surmised that the greatest problem facing the human race was—what?—heartburn. That was the season of the Great Heartburn Medication Wars.

Tagamet HB and Pepcid AC had just hit the market and Zantac 75 was on the horizon.

Television was consumed with commercials for these "acid blockers," pills that allowed you to overeat and overeat all the wrong things and still not feel that tinge of guilt or heartburn.

Is heartburn a major national health concern? Well, not exactly. How many people do you know who have died from it? How many 2 A.M. TV commercials have you seen for the National Heartburn Foundation?

Heartburn is an inconvenience. Which is not to say it isn't real or doesn't cause serious pain. But for most people, heartburn can be relieved by simply swallowing an antacid, say, a Rolaids or Tums tablet or a spoonful of Maalox or Di-Gel.

Zantac and Tagamet and Pepcid are a new category of heartburn medication: histamine H2 receptor antagonists. They were developed to treat ulcers and other stomach conditions involving excess acid. They are more powerful than run-of-the-mill antacids, which means you can really eat a lot of garbage and still sleep like a baby. The only problem with these acid blockers is that they don't work right away. So for Tagamet or Zantac to be effective you have to take them at least an hour before overeating. You have to plan your binges down at the local steak-and-grease house.

This isn't a problem for folks who overeat and suffer from acid indigestion. They are mostly older people, and if you've ever wandered into Ryan's Steakhouse at four in the afternoon, you know that these folks are good at planning their meals ahead. They've been waiting all afternoon for the place to open.

The over–fifty-five portion of the population consumes 58 percent of antacids.

A recent Gallup poll found that 44 percent of adults experience heartburn at least once a month, and 13 percent take indigestion medicine at least twice a week

Zantac—which was the original acid controller (AC) or H2 blocker (HB)—and its children have been a booming success in the short time they've been available without a prescription. Not that they weren't wildly successful in the prescription market. The prescription version of Zantac was the most-prescribed medication in America for the last five years before it went over-the-counter. In only six months in 1995, Tagamet and Pepcid added some $2,500 in sales to the average drugstore. And three months after it was introduced, Zantac 75 passed both Tagamet and Pepcid in sales.

Fast relief is the number-one thing consumers look for in an antacid, so Zantac et al. will never beat Rolaids et al. They've just made antacids a value-added category in the drugstore. People who count these things believe that by the year 2000 the antacid category should be turning about $1.6 billion a year, double the 1994 figure. Almost all of that projected growth will come from H2 blockers. And ten years ago no one had ever even heard of an H2 blocker.

Rogaine Update, Three Months Later

I went to the barbershop the other day and as I was settling in the chair, I looked at Garland, my barber of the last seven years, and said, "Don't take any off the top."

And he didn't laugh.

"Don't take any off the top." I haven't said that to a barber in twenty-five years.

I'm growing hair.

I never expected to be writing that sentence. In fact, I figured that by the third month of my experiment I would have nothing to write. I figured that after one month I could write that it was too early to say. After month two I could say "nothing so far." And for the fourth and final month, I could just write the whole thing off.

But I don't have to look up failure in the thesaurus.

I am growing hair.

After three months of twice-daily applications, the new over-the-counter drug Rogaine is working.

Now the downside: I am not growing a lot of hair. I have two long black hairs right up front, a bunch of long gray ones on the top and in the back, and longer fuzz everywhere else. But it's a start.

And now I'm really beginning to wonder if all that long fuzz will take off in the next thirty days. After all, the Rogaine bottle says to give it two to four months. This is only month three.

I have hair growing on the top of my head. The last time I could say that it wasn't growing in my ears, too.

I'm not just doing this for myself. I'm doing it for all mankind. And womankind.

I've had many more women ask how the experiment is going than men. They are all interested for their husbands and boyfriends.

I'm not the only one doing it either. I ran out of my first month's supply of Rogaine the week before Father's Day and I had a dickens of a time finding a new bottle. Everyone was sold out.

Is Rogaine the new Father's Day gift of choice?

9
The Privates:
Uh, Not About a Bunch of Soldiers and Their Misadventures in the Drugstore

This chapter is about those unmentionable products, the ones people sneak to the register and try to purchase before another customer arrives. And slink away when the clerk announces over the store PA, "Price check on condoms."

Trojan Large—12 Condoms—$5.95

Did Trojans use Trojans? Yes, they did. Not Trojan brand, of course, not "ultra-thin ribbed latex, lubricated with spermicide." But condoms were already in widespread use by the time of the Trojan civilization (1300 B.C.).

Did Trojans invent Trojans?

Naaaah. Condoms have been around longer than that. The ancient Egyptians—who predate the Trojans by a couple of millennia—had an early version of the condom, a sheath made from goat intestines. The purpose was not birth control but— like the filling-station rubber machines used to say—"sold for the prevention of disease only." Venereal disease was a real killer before the discovery of penicillin. Illegitimate children were nothing compared to death by sore crank.

An Italian guy named Gabriel Fallopius (he discovered the tube that bears his name, and what a wonderful time he must have had looking for it) developed a medicated version in the sixteenth century. It was eight inches in length and held on by a pink ribbon—the marketing department must have suggested that, female appeal and all.

Norman E. Himes, author of the definitive history of the condom, the 1936 tome *Medical History of Contraception,* says the first published mention of the condom is in Gabriel Fallopius's *De morbo gallico,* published in 1564. "If you fear lest syphilis be produced in the canal, take the sheath of this linen cloth and place it in the canal; I tried the experiment on eleven hundred men, and I call immortal God to witness that not one of them was infected." An added advantage, Fallopius noted, was that it fit in the pocket.

So how come it came to be called a condom instead of a fallopian tube (that name would have fit, too)? Some sources says the name came from the Earl of Condom, the royal physician to Britain's King Charles II, who ruled from 1660 to 1685. The earl developed a sheath of oiled sheep's intestine that kept the king frisky and infection free. According to this story, the device became known as Condom's sheath—a name the earl spent the rest of his life discouraging—and the name has passed down to the modern version, the latex prophylactic.

Himes tries to pooh-pooh the Dr. Condom tale, noting that the efforts of historians Frederick Ferdy and Havelock Ellis failed to turn up a record of such a physician. Himes says that neither of the two great diarists of the time, Samuel Pepys and

John Evelyn, ever mentioned Dr. Condom. He speculates it was the German syphilis expert Christoph Girtanner who started the rumor in a 1788 work. But even Himes is baffled by the origin of the word *condom*. Could it be Dr. Condom? "I am inclined to think it a myth; but confess that disproof is impossible. But neither is proof possible."

Yet another possibility bandied by the folks who bandy these sorts of things is that it comes from the French word *condus,* meaning "to conceal, protect, preserve." That's certainly the aim. Neither the French nor the English want to claim the word. The French call the condom *la capote anglaise*—"the English cape"—and the English refer to it as the "French letter."

Charles Goodyear received U.S. Patent No. 5,536 in 1848 for a process to manufacture hollow rubber articles and the rush was on for condom production. The vulcanized rubber condom first appeared sometime in the 1860s. It was a great improvement over the intestine sheath—both in smell and in providing pleasure.

The first mention of a rubber condom is in the 1858 edition of Robert Dale Owen's *Moral Physiology.* John Cowan's 1869 book *The Science of a New Life* described condoms made of rubber, but said that users complained that they dulled sensation and irritated the vagina. Cowan was probably accurate in his reporting. These early condoms were crude creations, made from sheet crepe with a seam running the length of the, uh, weapon.

A key advance in condom culture was the development of the seamless sheath. Once the technology for manufacturing seamless rubber products was developed, seamless condoms were the first order of business, even before the manufacture of seamless rubber gloves. This country has always had its priorities straight, hasn't it?

In Europe, condoms were sold in a number of retail outlets, including the barbershop and the grocery. In this country, because they were sold only for the prevention of disease—contraception was a word you seldom heard—condoms were introduced to the market via drugstores. An 1887 catalog for a Chicago wholesale drug supplier, Peter Van Schaack and Sons, called them "capotes" and sold them for seventy-five cents a dozen for white and fifty cents a dozen for pink.

Merrill Youngs, head of the Youngs Rubber Corporation, trademarked the Trojan name in 1926, when it was still illegal to sell condoms across state lines.

Youngs introduced quality control to the condom market, a concept not previously known or adhered to. When the FDA did a study on the subject in 1949, it found only two companies that met government standards for elasticity, elongation, thickness and strength. Youngs's Trojans, of course, and the Schmed Company's Ramses.

Youngs wasn't the only one to think of the Trojan metaphor for the condom—there's a surprise inside and not a good one—but he was the first one at the trademark office. His vigorous defense of the Trojan trademark led to his filing an infringement suit against a Chicago condom company, C. I. Lee, which was also selling a Trojan condom. From that lawsuit came a reinterpretation of the anticontraception laws, which led to a condom boom. Condom companies were manufacturing a million and a half a day in 1936. Sixty years later, that number has quadrupled.

Today, two companies command the lion's share of the condom business: Carter-Wallace and Schmed. Carter-Wallace owns the Trojan brand, which dominates with 56 percent of the condom market. Schmed's Ramses and Sheik brands combine for 34 percent of condom sales.

Would it surprise you to find out that the man who founded the number-two condom company, Schmed, Inc., started his working life as a sausage maker? Julius Schmed founded the company after working for years stuffing sausage. You have to wonder what he thought about all day long.

The modern condom is a scientific miracle, so thin that its presence is often unnoticed—ask a truck driver what one of those ladies at an interstate massage parlor can do—so inexpensive that the typical condom costs about a dime to manufacture and package, and so strong that ruptures are almost unheard of.

For that last trick—so to speak—thank the FDA. Government regulations say that a condom must be able to inflate to 1.5 cubic feet without bursting. That's about the size of an August watermelon. Inflate it that large and you could probably sell it to a junior high boy.

The typical drugstore carries forty different brands of condoms. That's less than half of the number produced by the major manufacturers. The 1996 *U.S. Pharmacopoeia* (*USP*) lists eighty-three different brand names of condoms, from Beyond Seven to Trojan Very Thin. It is instructive just to read the list: names like Class Act (do it in class?), Kimono (a little robe for Mr. Johnson?), Ramses (fit for a king or fits a king?) and Kling-Tite Natural Lamb. Yes, "Natural Lamb" means they are made from lamb cecum. For the layman in the crowd (got to get a good double entendre with *lay* in here somewhere), that is a sheep's intestines. Feel different about yourself now, Kling-Tite users?

There are twenty different Trojan brands, including Trojan Large. How large? The largest on the market, according to Condomania, a mail-order condom company. This model measures in at 214 millimeters long. If you're not reading this in Europe, that's 8.43 inches long.

And at 56 millimeters, it's also the widest condom (among condoms longer than 190 millimeters—there are wider condoms for the condom equivalent of the husky market). Translating for American soil, that's a diameter of 2.2 inches, which makes it bigger around than the Susan B. Anthony silver dollar.

Drugstores love rubbers. The profit margins are huge, in the neighborhood of 40 to 50 percent, making them one of the most profitable items in the store.

And despite years of stories about disapproving pharmacists, the drugstore is still the place where most people buy condoms. Americans spend about $240 million a year on condoms, and 75 percent of those purchases are in drugstores.

A sign that times have changed: 25 percent of condoms are purchased by women.

Condoms are no longer always kept behind the counter under the watchful eye of the druggist. They are now often out in the open. Very open. Drugstores actively promote their sale. In fact, *Drug Topics,* a trade magazine, advises drugstore owners, "In order to build business . . . cross-merchandise condoms. Additional locations for impulse sales include the front register, the men's toiletries department and the feminine hygiene department." Let's see, I need a pack of gum and a couple of batteries, and, oh yeah, slip me a pack of rubbers.

Ground zero for condoms is the Carter-Wallace plant in the Appomattox Industrial Center off Ruffin Mill Road in Chesterfield County, Virginia, near Richmond. That's where most of America's condoms are made, in hilly farmland. Where Robert E. Lee turned over his sword to Ulysses Grant, swordsmen of a different sort are being honored.

Despite years of technological advances, the *USP* says—and this will do nothing to comfort all those women whose men use condoms—"pregnancy occurs in 12 of each 100 women during the first year of condom use." Whoa.

The USP recommends against using oil-based "lubricants" (you know who you are) on condoms because "oil-based products such as hand, face or body cream, petroleum jelly, cooking oils or shortenings [insert whistle sound here]; or mineral or baby oil" weaken the latex rubber.

And finally these words of caution, again from the *USP,* and again, with a straight face: "Do not fill with water to check for leaks."

The pharmacy world is filled with funny stories about condom sales. I offer three here.

When David Inman of Jeffersonville, Indiana, was in high school, he used to make deliveries for his local drugstore. One customer called in an order for a toothbrush. Inman dutifully made the delivery. But when the man opened up his package, he blushed. Inside was a package of condoms. "My mother took the order. He had said he wanted a prophylactic toothbrush and she sent him out prophylactics."

Amy Moore of Cincinnati grew up in Baltimore and worked at a drugstore during high school. "Any time a young boy would come in acting all nervous, the pharmacist knew it was his first time. So when he asked for a pack of condoms, the pharmacist would always ask, 'What size?'"

And finally Eddie Rowe of Rowe's Pharmacy in Kingsport, Tennessee, tells the story of the confused stock boy at his store. "He was putting price stickers on all the merchandise and putting it out. When I went over to the condoms to see how he had done, I discovered he didn't know how to work the little pricing gizmo. He had priced the condoms a dollar a foot."

Kotex Curved Maxi-Pad—24 Pack—$2.98

The female cycle is not new. It's been around as long as there have been females. But public discourse about female plumbing is a relatively recent occurrence. In fact, if you make a timeline called Human Timeline (you can make it for the purposes of this book and reuse it in your social studies class) and the timeline is, say, ten feet long, then discourse about menstruation would occupy only the last inch.

It just wasn't talked about.

Women had periods before the advent of the television commercial, as proven by research conducted in 1927 by the industrial psychiatrist Dr. Lillian Gilbreth. She estimated that the typical woman menstruated for thirty-two years (from thirteen to forty-five) at an average of thirteen periods per year. That figured out to 416 periods per woman. Gilbreth was on assignment for Johnson & Johnson, the Band-Aid people, who were trying to introduce a new sanitary napkin.

In the history of feminine protection, Johnson & Johnson is sort of the Daniel Boone of the field. The company introduced Lister's Towels, a gauze-covered pad, to the sanitary napkin market, in 1894. The problem was, there was no sanitary napkin market in 1894.

Not that women didn't want, or need, a disposable sanitary napkin. Between 1854 and 1914 there were twenty different sanitary napkin patents granted by the U.S. government. At the time, most women used rags, which they washed out by hand after each use. That's where the saying "Don't air your dirty linens in public" came from.

The need was there. But Johnson & Johnson couldn't get the word out. No magazines, no newspapers, no media outlet in 1894 would accept an ad for the product.

You just didn't discuss the menses.

So the company tucked tail, so to speak, and discontinued the line. And then they watched from the sideline as the Kimberly-Clark company virtually stumbled into the market. During World War I, Kimberly-Clark had developed a cellulose wadding for wounds. This cellucotton was widely used in hospitals and first-aid stations and was particularly welcome because at the time, cotton was in short supply. Army nurses discovered they could cut the wadding and use it in place of a rag for their menstrual period.

When the war ended, there were tons of this cellucotton lying around in army storage facilities and Red Cross back rooms. Kimberly-Clark had a choice. It could buy the stuff back and maintain a market for it, or it could let the army dump it in the open market and watch the price of its product plummet. It decided to buy the surplus and figure out some use for it. That use turned out to be sanitary napkins.

But first, Kimberly-Clark formed a new company, International Cellucotton Corporation, to distance itself from what it feared might be a public backlash against marketing such a delicate product.

So in 1921 International Cellucotton entered the consumer market with this sanitary napkin it called Cellunap, short for cellucotton napkin. Huh? Next it hired an ad man whose first suggestion was to junk the name. He suggested combining the product's description—"cotton texture"—and creating a name: cotton textile became Kotex.

It still wasn't an easy sell.

No magazines would touch an ad. The first Kotex ad, a circumspect number, ran in 1921 in newspapers. That ad read: "To Save Men's Lives Science Discovered Kotex (Cotton Textile) A Wonderful Sanitary Absorbent." Nowhere did it say what it absorbed. Nor did the second ads, which also harked back to the war with a couple of nurses and a man in a wheelchair. The caption read, "At stores and shops that cater to women."

Groceries were afraid of the product, so too were general stores and even beauty shops.

And no woman would consider buying a box of sanitary napkins from a male druggist. So the first boxes of Kotex sat idly on the drugstore shelf. And sat and sat. Finally the company's ad man—a new ad man, Albert Lasker of Lord & Thomas—struck on the idea of self-serve. Package the napkins individually in plain wrappers, place them in boxes in a discreet back corner of the store, set a money box next to them, and hand letter a sign: HONOR SYSTEM. And that's how Kotex finally penetrated the market.

By 1927 they owned the market. Johnson & Johnson had a modest entry called Modess, but it was no big seller.

Enter Dr. Lillian Gilbreth.

If the name sounds familiar, it's because Gilbreth and her husband Frank were the parents in *Cheaper by the Dozen,* an affectionate family biography cowritten by one of their sons and one of their daughters. (And later turned into a charming Clifton Webb–Myrna Loy movie.)

She sent out 3,000 surveys and got 1,062 back. The results give us a rare picture of the way women thought about feminine protection in the twenties. Women listed comfort as the most important quality in a sanitary napkin. Second was adequate protection. Modesty didn't enter until number three: inconspicuousness. No tell-tale signs that a woman was having her period. Disposability ranked fourth and availability fifth. They weren't worried about where they could buy it: they would find it.

Gilbreth recommended that Johnson & Johnson not change the Modess name to Flush-Down (they were considering it), and she recommended a change in shape, to make Modess more comfortable. (She thought Kotex too bulky, and she was probably right; those first napkins were nine inches long, three and a half inches wide and had tapes extending an additional five and a half inches in front and seven and a half inches in back.)

She concluded that the sanitary napkin market had barely been tapped. She was right there. And she believed that napkins then on the market didn't satisfy consumers.

She recommended a major national health campaign on the subject of menstruation. I think that's probably where the Johnson & Johnson people quit reading. No such major effort was in the offing. Instead, the sanitary napkin slowly eased its way into the marketplace.

The big breakthrough came in 1924 when ad man Lasker

convinced Ed Bok, the editor of *Ladies' Home Journal,* to accept an ad. He did it by bringing Bok's secretary into the discussion. Let her decide if the ads are in good taste. She said they were, and the floodgates were open.

Today, sanitary protection is a $1.6 billion industry with drugstores grabbing $410.6 million of that total, about one-fourth. There are no more honor-system boxes. Women feel no embarrassment carrying a giant Kotex box through the Wal-Mart if they can get a better price there. Men don't even mind buying for their wives. Well, we mind a little bit.

That $1.6 billion sanitary protection market is evenly split between napkins and tampons. The new number-one name in napkins belongs to Johnson & Johnson: it's Stayfree, the adhesive-backed napkin. And the name in tampons is Tampax.

Tampax was developed in 1931 by a country doctor named Earl Haas. He got the idea after treating many women who hated the bulky, chafing pads. Not that the idea was new. Women had been creating their own since Egyptian women made them from water-soaked papyrus. Haas got a patent for his invention, which he named the "catamenial device," from the Greek word for "monthly." The invention was better than the name. It was compressed cotton with a string for easy and sanitary removal and a cardboard tube for easy and sanitary insertion. Haas created a new name for the marketplace, combining the ancient name for the device, tampon, with "vaginal pack" to get "Tampax."

It was the height of the Depression, and Haas could never get anyone to manufacture his invention. So in 1933, he threw up his hands and sold out to a Denver doctor, Gertrude Tenderich. She put together a group of investors and took Tampax to market in 1934. Sort of. Like Kotex before it, Tampax met much resistance. The preachers denounced it. The media ignored it. It wasn't until she hooked up with New York financier Ellery Mann that she was able to combat the charges. He sold Tampax as a doctor's invention that had even been "accepted for advertising by the American Medical Association," a boast that was true, if meaningless. Tampax went national in 1936 with the slogan "No belts. No pins. No pads." In 1937 Tampax made a profit, and it has been making one ever since.

The burning question is, how did they ever convince that first woman to use a tampon? The first users weren't concerned about, well, health issues, like toxic shock syndrome. They were worried about what others would think if they stuffed a . . . never mind. So Tampax began packing a little instruction sheet in each box. Still do. It includes a question-and-answer section that's designed to alleviate the fears of Catholic schoolgirls everywhere. The key question is addressed in the first sentence: "*Tampons do not affect virginity* (my emphasis). The hymen has an opening large enough to allow menstrual fluid out, and a tampon easily slips through that same opening."

So you can be a virgin and use a tampon.

Ex-Lax, Chocolated—48 Count—$7.49

I have a pharmacist friend—let's call him David and make everyone whose pharmacist is named David nervous—and when David was in pharmacy school, he decided to conduct an experiment. Nothing new here—pharmacy school is full of adventuresome scientific types. But David's experiment was new. And it might have made the journals had he conducted it under more rigorous testing conditions.

David wondered which worked faster—a laxative or an antidiarrheal. So he took Ex-Lax and Immodium-AD at the same time.

The results of that experiment in a moment.

The laxative section of the drugstore is not the hot section. Laxative sales are declining. People aren't battling to get the last box of that hot new constipation killer. And it's not just because the prime users of laxatives are older people, although that's certainly a part of it. It's that there have been no breakthrough products in the thousands of years since Hippocrates wrote down his cathartic formula. Also there are no new uses for Ex-Lax, no studies suggesting laxatives also prevent heart attack, no Cepacol of constipation. That happened with aspirin, you recall, when scientists said it could help prevent heart attacks and sent aspirin sales, which had also been declining for years, soaring.

Sales of "laxatives and stool softeners"—isn't this a wonderful product category?—are declining for good reason. The category is being battered from all sides. No innovation, no breakthrough, and lately more people have been combating irregularity—as the TV commercials call it—with dietary measures, including eating more fiber.

Laxatives have their customers, to be sure: one-fourth of people aged fifty-five to sixty-four use laxatives and a third of those sixty-five and older use them.

The typical drugstore sells $12,000 a year in laxatives, which is nothing to make annoying flatulent sounds about. And there is a nice profit margin on them. Drugstores can pretty much charge whatever they want for products in this category, because, as *Drug Topics* delicately put it, "Customers usually purchase laxatives and stool softeners to cure constipation *after* it has become a reality. These customers want prompt results and aren't as likely to shop for the best prices."

That's right. It's hard to comparison shop when you are doubled over in pain.

Laxatives date back to the earliest drug manuals, or stone tablets—we've always known the benefits of a good dump. And the agony of irregularity.

So what is regularity?

Well, according to the groundbreaking 1996 study *Bowel habit in relation to age and gender: findings from the National Health Interview Survey and clinical implications,* it's roughly—and I use that adjective with trepidation—a dump a day. Of the 40,000 people surveyed, "83.4 percent reported at least one bowel movement per day." There, we've got it out in the open. The study's authors further state that 94 to 99 percent of both young and old people report at least three bowel movements per week.

If you're wondering about that gender gap, yes, there is one: "Women reported generally fewer bowel movements per week than men."

The study found a direct relationship between advancing age and laxative use, which is news only to people who don't have a grandmother. One-third of all respondents eighty and over use a laxative or stool softener at least once a month. This compares to only 6 percent of people younger than forty.

The good news for those of us who are getting older—and if you are getting younger, please contact the study's authors so they can study you—is that "despite conventional wisdom, bowel movement frequency does not generally decline with advancing age."

Other gems from this study:

- 5.9 percent of people under forty had two or fewer bowel movements a week.
- 3.8 percent of those aged sixty to sixty-eight had two or fewer bowel movements a week.
- 6.0 percent of those eighty and over had two or fewer bowel movements a week.

Ex-Lax is another pharmacist's contribution to pharmaceuticals. It was created around the turn of the century by Max Kiss, a Hungarian native, who got the idea when he was celebrating his graduation from pharmacy school with a visit back to the old country. On board the ship, he heard a number of doctors talking about a new tasteless powder, phenolphthalein, developed by the German aspirin company Friedrich Bayer. It had been used for years to test the acidity in wine, but one day a wine-tester looked around to see that all of his colleagues were "down the hall." Kiss went home, mixed phenolphthalein in chocolate and—hey—it worked.

Kiss initially called his creation Bo-Bo, but fortunately he spotted a Hungarian newspaper headline about a deadlock in parliament, which the paper labeled ex-lax (which is Hungarian for a deadlock in parliament). Kiss put two and two together—excellent-laxative—and had his new name. And new career.

Back to my friend David the pharmacist. You remember David, the guy who took Ex-Lax and Immodium-AD at the same time to see which would win the race to his intestines.

Uh, Ex-Lax won.

Sal Hepatica—4 Suppositories—$3.98

Sal Hepatica—wasn't he the third baseman for the Philadelphia Phillies Whiz Kids, the pennant winners of 1950? It sure seems like it. Actually Sal Hepatica was a mineral salt laxative that was popular about the time the Phillies were having that pennant run. It was one of many nostrums cited as ineffective in Peter Morell's 1937 muckraking book *Poisons, Potions and Profits.*

The formula has been changed. Today Sal is a sodium phosphate laxative, same as a number of other brands, including Fleet Phospho-Soda and Fleet Enema.

Sal Hepatica is available in liquid or enema form, which sets it apart from products like the Ex-Lax and Feen-A-Mint, which are only sold as tablets. The enema form works in five to ten minutes. Sal Hepatica, the old Phillie third baseman, was quick, but he wasn't that quick.

Preparation H—1-Ounce Tube—$5.79

The question shouldn't be, What is Preparation H? The question should be, What were Preparations A through G? What was wrong with them? Okay, okay, Preparation H is just a name. There were no preparations A through G, according to the folks who make Preparation H. The H signifies what the preparation is supposed to cure: hemorrhoids.

Preparation H, is, or *was,* until recently, live yeast cell derivative (LYCD), a compound that would shrink tissue indiscriminately. Then the government, which makes it its business to protect us from charlatan hemorrhoid cures, ruled that Preparation H was completely ineffective in treating hemorrhoids.

Preparation H had satisfied generations of hemorrhoid sufferers when the government banned its active ingredient, the yeast cell derivative, in 1994, claiming that "two submitted studies did not adequately support claims that LYCD effectively treats hemorrhoid symptoms such as pain, itching, burning or irritation or swollen tissues caused by inflammation."

But rather than pull its product from the market—it sells $100 million a year in Preparation H ointments, creams, towelettes and suppositories—Preparation H's manufacturer, Whitehall, just altered the formula. Goodbye yeast, hello shark liver oil. Hello, *what?* That's right. Now one of the active ingredients is shark liver oil. But before you laugh, when have you ever heard a shark complain about a hemorrhoid?

How does it work? Essentially, Preparation H is supposed to shrink tissue. That doesn't get rid of a hemorrhoid, but it can decrease the pain. And that shrinking property isn't just limited to hemorrhoids. It will shrink any tissue. In Florida, many older

Preparation H purchasers buy it to use as a sort of instant face-lift.

Preparation H has the distinction of being one of the most frequently stolen items in the drugstore, according to the folks at Sensormatic, who make those little antitheft tags that set off alarms every time some old woman wanders through a Sensormatic gate while trying to get at some other merchandise.

Why steal Preparation H? It's not like it's a big-ticket item. Well, some people are just too embarrassed to buy it. After all, buying this in the drugstore is the same as telling the clerk "my butt hurts." Probably not the best way to make a new friend and certainly not recommended as a pick-up line.

But lots of people's butts hurt: one in three, according to government research. And how do they do this research? I don't want to think about it. Let's think instead about the little magnetic tags that thwart crime—and cut down on Preparation H–lifting.

The industry leader in antitheft tags is Sensormatic Electronics of Deerfield Beach, Florida. In 1996, the company sold more than 3 billion of those little fingernail-sized magnetic tags. Other companies are in the security tag business—Checkpoint Systems, Knogo Corporation and 3M among them—but Sensormatic is the giant of the industry. Checkpoint is trying to catch up. It recently signed on with Walgreens and Thrift Drug. Next time you go into a drugstore, look on those little aluminum threshold arches, and chances are it will say Sensormatic.

Sensormatic says Preparation H is just one of the hot five, the hottest items in the drugstore—literally hot, as in stolen. The other frequently filched items are batteries, cosmetics, film and sunglasses.

I don't see a pattern there.

Pampers Disposable Diapers, Size 3— 84 Diapers—$18.98

Here's what people think they know about disposable diapers:

Disposable Diapers Common Knowledge #1—The landfills are mountained with millions of turd-filled disposable diapers, causing a landfill crisis in this country.

Disposable Diapers Common Knowledge #2—Disposable diapers are more expensive than cloth diapers.

Disposable Diapers Common Knowledge #3—Cloth diapers are better for baby and baby's tender skin.

Disposable Diapers Common Knowledge #4—Disposable diapers were invented because yuppies were too lazy to wash diapers.

For expert knowledge on disposable diapers let's turn not to an industry spokesperson with an axe to grind, but to a person on the front lines. Dr. Susan Boiko, a pediatric dermatologist, presented a paper on diapering to the American Dermatology Association in 1995. Here's what she said about the first three of those firmly held beliefs.

1. Disposable diapers make up 1 to 2 percent of landfills, not the 50 percent frequently cited. They are not clogging up the dumps, turning our landfills from land to fills.
2. If you wash them, cloth diapers are cheaper; if you use a service, the cost is about the same.
3. If you can't change baby's wet diaper soon after soiling, disposables are better. They hold moisture away from the

skin, decreasing the chances that baby's skin will become irritated and develop a rash.

Diapers have been around for centuries. In the Bible, the baby Jesus was wrapped in swaddling clothes, an early form of the diaper. Through the ages, linen strips were the diaper material of choice, at least for those who could afford them.

Now, about that fourth bit of common knowledge: Disposable diapers come directly from the fact that one grandpa hated washing those messy old cloth diapers. That one grandpa was Vic Mills, a researcher in the development department at Procter & Gamble in Cincinnati. After a stint babysitting his grandson, Mills vowed there had to be a better way and assigned some of his top people to look into disposable diapers.

There were already a number of disposable diapers on the market when Mills had his epiphany in 1956. There were Chux and Drypers and Kleinerts and K.D.'s, but they made up only 1 percent of the diaper changes in this country. They were mainly a product for vacationers and travelers. Chux ads from the time highlighted the fact: "For the family outing."

Disposable diapers were not an immediate hit because mothers didn't like them. They were cumbersome, they leaked and they were expensive. But 1956 was the heart of the baby boom. There were babies everywhere. Disposable diapers were a product waiting to happen.

Mills's researchers originally worked on an absorbent pad to insert in a special plastic panty. That design was already used in Scandinavia. P&G test-marketed this early version of the disposable diaper in Dallas in the summer of 1958. But the resultant heat rashes from the plastic pants nearly doomed the project. In March 1959, P&G tried again, this time in Rochester, New York, using two designs: one mothers taped on, the other they pinned on. This time the diapers were a hit. Now the marketing department went to work on a name. They tried Tads and Solos and Larks before settling on Pampers.

P&G, ever the cautious conglomerate, tried a full-scale market test in Peoria later that same year. Pampers didn't play in Peoria. At ten cents a diaper—in 1959, a family of four could eat at McDonald's for that, provided they shared a sack of fries and drank water—it was a failure. But P&G kept testing, and at six cents their diaper was a hit.

Hello, Pampers! Hello, Luvs and Huggies and store brand!

Try buying a cloth diaper today. Try finding a cloth diaper service. It's not easy.

The secret to the disposable's success is that it works. After years of tweaking, the conglomerates have come up with a three-layer design: the outer plastic, the absorbent wadding and—the secret to the success—the porous sheet that allows baby's pee to pass through but not to seep back on baby.

P&G's Luvs brand introduced the hourglass shape and elastic legs to the disposable diaper market in 1980. Kleenex's Huggies brand, introduced that same year, added a wider waist tape and the polypropylene liner that allowed baby's wetness to pass through to the absorbent filler but not pass back on baby. Luvs and Huggies were both premium diapers, with a premium price some 30 percent above Pampers. Kleenex's Huggies might never have survived—it might have been smothered in the cradle by the marketing might of P&G—had not P&G spent such an extraordinary length of time test-marketing Luvs: two and one-half years.

About the only downside to disposables, according to Dr. Boiko, is that babies will eat them if they are left nearby. But then babies will also eat crayons or safety pins or just about anything that is left in reach. The lesson here may be to keep everything out of baby's grasp. Dr. Boiko also stresses that using the proper size diaper is important. A too-tight diaper can cut or chafe.

The disposable-diaper companies have been listening to Dr. Boiko, too. Disposables now come in five sizes, assorted absorbencies, different cuts, even different styles for boys and girls. If I have to tell you how boys' diapers differ from girls', you don't need to be buying disposable diapers anyway.

Charmin Ultra Toilet Paper—4-Roll Pack—$1.38

To paraphrase Mark Twain's famous remark about blushing: Man is the only animal who wipes himself. Or needs to.

And thus . . . toilet paper.

There was toilet paper long before there was *toilet paper.* Why do you think the Sears catalog was so popular among farm families? You think they were all that interested in J. C. Higgins washing machines and Silvertone golf clubs? No. They used last year's catalog for this year's toilet paper.

But that's rather late in the evolution of wiping.

Ancient civilizations varied in the civility with which they treated the wiping function. The Romans had saltwater sponges on sticks in all their public toilets. The rich Romans, who didn't use public toilets anyway, preferred rosewater-soaked wool for their wiping.

Less civilized civilizations used whatever was handy—literally. That meant wiping with seashells or leaves or sticks. Or in the really uncivilized civilizations, what was handy was the hand, the bare hand. Some believe this is where the tradition of shaking right hands came from. You see, the left hand was the wiping hand.

Guttenberg was the father of toilet paper. In his own way. He made printed matter ubiquitous, and, for many, *ubiquitous* translated to *handy*.

Down on the farm, the corncob was still king. And would be until Mr. Sears and Mr. Roebuck made their catalogs ubiquitous. The Sears catalog was popular for outhouses until 1934, when Mr. Sears and Mr. Roebuck switched from newsprint to coated paper. Not a pretty sight. Or feel.

But toilet paper, of any variety, didn't become a household product until the invention of the flushing toilet in 1884 by one Thomas Crapper. (That was his real name.) Corncobs just didn't go down the crapper all that easily. People needed something small, disposable and—it had taken a few millennia to establish this—soft!

Enter the Scott brothers of Saratoga, New York. They began manufacturing a product they called Waldorf Tissue. It really was more what we think of as tissue. It came in a box, not on a roll. And they named it after Manhattan's ritzy Waldorf-Astoria Hotel because they assumed no one would be willing to pay for toilet tissue except a hotel.

They advertised that their tissue was "soft as old linen," an apt comparison because at the time that was what royalty used for wiping.

Scott was pretty much the name in toilet paper until 1957,

when soap giant Procter & Gamble bought the Charmin Paper Mills of Green Bay, Wisconsin, and began a toilet paper war.

P&G, one of the most market-oriented companies in America, discovered from its marketing research department that Americans wanted a softer, more durable toilet paper. Take it on faith. You don't want to see the questionnaire.

At the time, toilet tissue, despite the name *tissue,* was closer to newsprint. It was a tad coarse. P&G changed the way Charmin made toilet paper, air-drying the finished product rather than squeeze-pressing it dry. It made all the difference in the world. It really was softer.

To impress this difference upon the public, P&G's advertising department came up with one of the most memorable advertising characters in history: Mr. Whipple. Mr. Whipple was a supermarket manager who had to keep telling customers, "Please, don't squeeze the Charmin." No one was squeezing the Charmin before that ad, but soon folks really were squeezing toilet paper in the supermarket. And, to P&G's delight, also buying it.

Premarin—12 Capsules—$15.98

It's sometimes easy to forget, as we lose ourselves in a sea of cosmetics and magazines, candy and aspirin, that the reason we have drugstores is for prescriptions. You can buy lipstick at the department store and magazines at the bookstore, candy at the convenience mart and aspirin at the grocery. But only a licensed pharmacist can fill a prescription.

Prescriptions are why drugstores exist. For the typical drugstore, prescriptions make up 40 percent of business, and druggists don't forget, not when they do the books. In 1996, pharmacists filled 2.4 billion prescriptions, worth a total of $78 billion. And that number is growing every year. In the sixties, seventies and eighties the number of prescriptions grew at only 1 percent annually. But in 1994, for the first time in decades, it jumped 2 percent.

What happened? Baby boomers, that giant population bulge of folks born between 1946 and 1962, suddenly hit middle age with a vengeance. And a backache. This number will only increase as baby boomers become seniors.

The most-prescribed drug in 1995, the last year for which this information is available, was Premarin, an estrogen compound that is prescribed to prevent postmenopausal osteoporosis. Baby boomer women are hitting menopause.

Second was Zantac, the ulcer and indigestion pill. Third was Synthroid, a thyroid medication. Rounding out the top five were Amoxil, an antibiotic, and Lanoxin, a heart drug that's also used to treat water retention and fatigue.

That was a slip for Zantac, which had been the most-prescribed drug for most of the fifteen years since it had been introduced in 1981. But it was a slip only in prescription rankings. Zantac became available without a prescription during 1995 and quickly leaped to the top of the over-the-counter sales chart.

Antibiotics and cardiovasculars were the most-prescribed category of drugs, with a 14.1 percent share. Second were psychotropics—Prozac, Valium and the like—with 8.8 percent. Analgesics—pain-relievers—ranked third, with a 7.8 percent share. Cough and cold medicines were fourth, with 4.2 percent.

Lydia Pinkham's Herbal Compound—
12-Ounce Liquid—$8.98

The names evoke chuckles today: Daffy's Elixir Selvitis, Lee's Bilious Pills, Widow Sarah Read's Well Known Ointment for the Itch. But when patent medicines took the country by storm in the nineteenth century, they were a boon to a health-care system that had its share of quacks and sophists.

The major treatment for disease until well after the Civil War was bleeding: opening a vein and letting it flow. To be sure, this reduced hypertension, then thought to be the one disease with many symptoms—it's hard to have high blood pressure when you don't have much blood, period. But it was a classic example of the cure that kills.

The most popular medicine at the time was calomel—mercury! Orthodox physicians of the nineteenth century regularly used treatments we now consider barbaric: vomiting, colon cleansing (sometimes by laxative, sometimes by enema), mercury poisoning and leeching, an extreme form of bleeding. Leeches, little blood-sucking worms, were attached to the skin and allowed to suck away. A man who could supply these parasitic worms could make a good living. Doctors even attached leeches to a woman's cervix.

Women in particular were at the mercy of these barbaric treatments. Even though Dutch doctor Regner de Graff had shown two centuries earlier that menstruation was tied to the production of eggs by the ovaries, doctors still viewed a woman's period as a time of sickness and referred to the uterus as the "sewer of all the excrements existing in the body."

It was into this medical system that patent medicines were born.

The first proprietary-medicine ad—that's actually a more correct term than "patent medicine" because the medicines were seldom patented but their labels were trademarked—appeared in a 1708 edition of the *Boston News-Letter*. The ad, paid for by Nicholas Boone Apothecary, was for Daffy's Elixir Selvitis, a compound senna tincture that worked as a laxative. The creator was a British clergyman, Reverend Daffy, who had concocted the elixir around 1650.

By the time Widow Sarah Read advertised her Well Known Ointment for the Itch in her son-in-law Ben Franklin's penny paper shortly before the Revolutionary War, proprietary medicines were becoming all the rage. The first to actually receive a patent under the new constitution was Lee's Bilious Pills, patented in 1796 and sold under the sign of the American eagle.

Patent-medicine sales took off in the new century—the nineteenth century.

Perhaps the most famous patent medicine of all, an elixir that was a drugstore staple up into the seventies—the 1970s!—was Lydia E. Pinkham's Vegetable Compound.

Lydia Pinkham was a New Englander. Her family's fortunes had been decimated by the panic of 1873—oh, that panic of '73—and her boys were looking for a way to help Mom and Pop out. Pop, you see, was the one who had lent freely in the good times before the panic.

The family had owned the vegetable compound recipe for years. It was either Liddy's own concoction, adapted from a medical pharmaceutical book of the day, or it was the only thing Pop left the family, a result of another of his generous loans. According to that story—certainly the more interesting—the recipe came from one George Clarkson Todd, a Lynn, Massachusetts, machinist who borrowed twenty-five dollars from Isaac Pinkham and paid off his debt with this secret recipe.

Actually, history should probably hope that the formula came from Mr. Todd. It could have come from Liddy's diary, which had a section she labeled "Medical Directions for Ailments." Her remedy for asthma called for "a hog's milt procured fresh from the slaughter house, split in halves, one half to be bound on the sole of each foot and allowed to remain there until perfectly dry."

Whatever its source, this vegetable compound was reputed to cure "female complaints," which covered a wide range of symptoms and were apparently the major cause of family discord at the time. Mom's spells, you know, that sort of thing.

The vegetable compound was a simple recipe: unicorn root, life root, black cohosh, pleurisy root and fenugreek seed. It was all soaked in what, a century later, appears to be the real secret ingredient: a 19 percent alcohol solution. This was as a preservative, of course, but preserving what, may be the better question.

Not that nice old Lydia Pinkham was promoting the use of alcohol. She herself was a member in good standing of the Women's Christian Temperance Union. I mean, you had to suspend all that mush in something.

The genius of Lydia's compound was in the marketing. Son Dan carried fliers down to Brooklyn, but the folks there wouldn't even take one, because the words "prolapsed uterus" were on the front. So he came up with a new, more ingenious marketing strategy. He had business cards printed up. Then on the back, he handwrote a message, making it appear it was to a third party: "Try Lydia E. Pinkham's Vegetable Compound. I know it will cure you; it's the best thing for Uterine complaints there is. Your Cousin, Mary." Then he dropped the cards at random on park benches and trolley stops, hoping people would pick them up, read them and rush out to the store to stock up. Some folks did.

Next, he tried newspaper ads. They worked, but they still weren't the breakthrough. The breakthrough came when they put Lydia's picture on the label. No one had ever done that before, put a female's photo on a label.

Lydia was not the Cindy Crawford of her day. For one thing, she was sixty. She looked like your worst aunt on her best day, a stern woman, with what couldn't even be described as a hint of a smile. But she was a stern woman for stern times.

With her graying hair in a pinched bun, her lips were pursed in a way that spoke volumes to the women of her day. Her photo said, "My female organs hurt, help me." Lydia Pinkham had an evangelistic look, and she was an evangelist for her vegetable compound. Sales of the vegetable compound boomed.

Newspapers aided her cause. Any time they needed a quick photo of a mature woman, they ran her photo. What readers would know Mrs. Pinkham from Queen Victoria or the actress Lily Langtry anyway?

Lydia was, as best we can figure out at this late date, the first woman used in an ad. The Smith brothers were famous for their cough drops; Buffalo Bill Cody was famous for his Wild West Show. But no woman had ever graced an ad.

Six months after that first ad, the Pinkhams were offered $100,000 for their business and the new trademark with Lydia's picture. They turned down the offer, and by 1881, they were selling $200,000 worth of vegetable compound a year.

For every action there is a reaction, and the success of patent medicines brought a call for a congressional investigation. What were these tonics? Charles Fletcher, manufacturer of Fletcher's Gentle Castoria, a laxative, told *The New York Times* in 1892: "If the [patent medicine] business were an underhanded one or if in the preparation of these articles, injurious substances were used, or if there were anything in the nature of fraud in respect to a large proportion of the well-known proprietary articles, there might be some excuse for special legislation against the manufacturers. No such excuse now exists."

Still, where there's a congressional rumble, there's usually a bill, and on June 30, 1906, Teddy Roosevelt signed the first Food and Drug Act, a piece of legislation spurred mostly by *The Jungle,* Upton Sinclair's muckraking novel about the meatpacking industry. Patent-medicine makers in general, and Lydia Pinkham's people in particular, through the Proprietary Association, fought hard to defeat the bill. But in the end, they benefited, because the bill gave them a respectability they had never enjoyed. Now their products seemed "regulated," although about the only restriction was that if the label stated that a product contained a certain ingredient, it was required to have that ingredient. You could still sell narcotics under the guise of Baby's Soothing Syrup, so long as you listed the narcotic on the label. At least Mom would know she was merely drugging the baby, not curing her.

By 1928, the sales of patent and proprietary medicines had doubled from pre-law days. Lydia Pinkham's Vegetable Compound was the best-selling patent medicine in the land.

Then in 1933 came a bill to upgrade the drug laws. This time Congress really did go after drug makers. It took them five years to put together the Food, Drug and Cosmetic Act, signed January 25, 1938. The bill caused a number of companies to modify their formulas and redesign their labels and advertising. But the patent-medicine craze continued unabated. It still does, despite a Nader-era reform movement that rid Carter of its little liver pills and sent Geritol reeling toward the retirement home.

Lydia E. Pinkham's Vegetable Compound was a success for almost a century. But times change. By 1979, a decade after the company had been bought by Cooper Laboratories, sales had fallen to $700,000 a year. It was too old fashioned with that old lady's picture on it. Plus the name vegetable compound paled next to such modern-sounding concoctions as Bufferin and Midol, two competitors.

Today, Lydia E. Pinkham's Vegetable Compound is still around, but now called Herbal Compound, and available in tablets and liquid form. But few urban drugstores stock it. You have to go to rural communities, where you'll find it on the shelf next to Black Draught. But that's another story.

The top patent medicines in 1996, by category:

1. Analgesics (pain relievers)
2. Laxatives
3. Vitamins
4. Cold and cough remedies
5. Antacids and stomach remedies
6. Antiseptics
7. Liniments
8. Tonics

If you want to engage your friendly local pharmacist in conversation, the easiest way is to inquire if he carries Lydia E.

Pinkham's Herbal Compound. The usual response goes something like this: "Man, I haven't seen that for years. Used to be we couldn't keep that stuff on the shelves. Wonder if they still sell it." He will then make a quick trip to his drug catalog. "Yeah, here it is. We're showing our age, talking about Lydia Pinkham." I've had that conversation with about fifty pharmacists in the last year.

Caution: it won't work on fuzzy-cheeked pharmacists.

First Response Home Pregnancy Kit—$11.98

If you think "The rabbit died" is a line from *Who Framed Roger Rabbit?* then you are from the younger generation. That was once the punchline for a hundred pregnant-girlfriend jokes. It referred to the rabbit test, a now-archaic method of determining whether or not a woman was pregnant.

The rabbit test was known more properly as Friedman's test, named for Maurice Friedman, an American physician who modified the old Aschheim-Zondek pregnancy test. For Friedman's test, a physician took a urine sample from the woman who suspected she was pregnant. This urine was then injected into a mature, virgin rabbit. Several days later, the rabbit was cut open and the ovaries inspected. If they contained fresh corpora lutea or hemorrhaging corpora, the woman was pregnant. The rabbit didn't die from the pregnancy, but from the surgery. The rabbit died, whether or not the woman was pregnant. It was sacrificed for the greater good.

Since the early eighties, teenagers and married women alike have been using in-the-privacy-of-your-own-home pregnancy tests to determine if that little celebration produced a little Oops.

The most popular brand of home pregnancy test is Lifescan, with a 14.1 percent share of the market. Early Pregnancy—as blunt a name as any in the drugstore—is second, with 9.5 percent. Rounding out the top five are Clearblue Easy, with 6.5 percent, Fact Plus, with 5.7 percent, and First Response, which sounds like a smoke detector, with 4.5 percent.

These home pregnancy tests work on a principle similar to that of the rabbit test—a fetus sloughs off cells and these live cells show up in the urine—but no rabbits are harmed in the process.

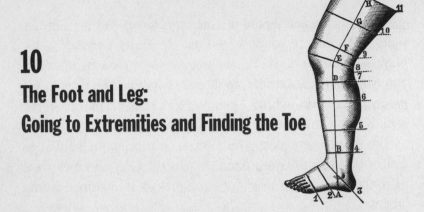

10
The Foot and Leg:
Going to Extremities and Finding the Toe

Drugstores sold $237.6 million worth of foot-care products in 1996. That money was split, just about down the middle, into two categories: athlete's foot medications and foot-care devices, most of the latter being Dr. Scholl's products. Because when most people think of the foot, they think of Dr. Scholl.

Dr. Scholl's Corn Remover—9 Discs—$3.08

Who is Dr. Scholl and what is this foot fetish of his? Everyone recognizes the familiar yellow-and-black label for Dr. Scholl's products, but who knows who Dr. Scholl was? Or even is? Or even if he was—or is—real? Unlike Aunt Jemima and Betty Crocker, Dr. Scholl was the real deal, a real doctor and a real foot freak.

Dr. Scholl was born William M. Scholl in 1882, an Indiana farm boy who had a near-fatal foot attraction.

His foot fetish came naturally: his grandfather was a shoemaker. His propensity for invention also had a genetic root—his father was a wagon maker who was always tinkering with his tools.

Young Willy taught himself shoemaking by completing 132,000 stitches a day! You think this guy had an obsession? He doesn't exactly sound like prime timber to marry your daughter off to.

At age sixteen, Scholl got a job in a Hammond, Indiana, shoe store and learned the art of shoe fitting. He saw that shoes were made on a mold that had little resemblance to the human foot and instantly recognized that that was why so many people had foot problems. At seventeen, he moved to Chicago and landed a job at Ruppert's Shoe Store, studying medicine at night and inventing foot supports in his spare time.

As a young physician, he walked the streets of Chicago with the skeletal remains of a pair of feet in the pockets of his frock coat. You can imagine how excited shoe stores must have been to see him at the door. He went from store to store on a mission: to convince shoe salesmen that feet didn't have to hurt, not with his handy-dandy triple-spring arch inserts.

The springs made the support self-adjusting. And when one customer exclaimed, "That's a real foot easer," Scholl knew he had a name. He trademarked the invention as the Foot-Eazer.

After graduation he rented a small cubbyhole space, set up a bed in the back and opened up shop. He stayed up late working on foot things, and by the end of his first month in business— June 1904—he had made $815.65, a tidy sum for the time. (Roughly equivalent to the national debt today.)

He took out a newspaper ad offering to cure "Tired Feet," and the public responded. This was in the days before doctors were opposed to advertising. In fact, the only trouble Scholl had was with a few publishers who objected to the drawing of a foot that he included in every ad. Please, no naked feet in a family publication, they said. In his spare time, he hotfooted it around to local shoe stores selling his Foot-Eazer. In 1907, gross sales were $17,373.69, and he was well on his way to becoming *the* name in foot products.

The next year he developed his first corn pad, a molded rubber cup held to the corn by adhesive tape. Because no air or moisture could reach the corn, it would separate from the skin and fall off. He called them Absorbo Pads, a name that perpetuated his string of strange-sounding foot inventions.

His tinkering continued, and he produced new foot products at the rate of about six a year, everything from bunion pads, for protection, not removal, to Toe Flex, a rubber bar worn between the toes and designed to straighten the big toe.

His first national ad appeared in a 1919 issue of *The Saturday Evening Post*:

> Rest for tired aching feet. Bodily aches—pains and foot ailments due to weak or breaking down arch instantly relieved by wearing Scholl's Foot-Eazers—supports the arch in an easy natural manner, removes nervous and muscular strain. Makes walking or standing restful. Scholl's Foot-Eazers are worn in any shoe—self adjusting, light, effective. Price $2 per pair.

There's more, lots, lots more. This is, after all, a man with boundless energy. I don't have space to discuss all of Dr. Scholl's innovations nor his place in history. If you want more, much more, read his biography, called, appropriately, *Feet First* (Scholl, Inc., 1972).

Schick Slim Twin Blade Razor for Ladies— 10-Pack—$3.98

Here's something I've been wondering about for twenty-five years: If the first blade pulls the hair out and then the second snips it off, why not a Triple Blade Razor? The first blade could pull the hair out, then the second blade could pull it out a little farther and then the third blade could snip it off. Or maybe a Quadruple Blade Razor? The first blade, then the second blade and then the third blade keep pulling out the hair for the fourth blade to whack it off. This concept would be limited only by how heavy a razor you could hold. (Or by our familiarity with Latin roots: Octuple Blade Razor is probably the limit on what the marketing people could sell.) Weight lifters and NFL linemen would have the smoothest legs in the country.

Seriously, is there anything more useless than shaving one's legs? Or more disgusting if you don't? But women have been doing this for a long, long time.

In the beginning men did it, too. Neanderthals used sharpened rocks or shells to scrape the hair from their legs. Anthropologists think this was to prevent lice—at least back then they had a reason.

Smooth, hairless legs became a beauty regimen in ancient Arabia. And a painful one, too; women laced string around their fingers, a variation on the cat's cradle, to grab the leg hairs and jerk them out. Ouch! But that was nothing compared to those eighteenth-century European women, who used caustic lye to burn the hair away. Ouch! Ouch! Ouch! Ouch!

There's probably never been a group so glad to see a technological advance. That came in the nineteenth-century with the invention of the stainless-steel razor. Since then it's been all smooth shaving.

Women spend $300 million annually on shaving products, most of it on twin-blade safety razors. And yes, there is a difference between a woman's razor and a man's. It's the handle. The ladies' razors have a sharper curve in the handle because women are more interested in seeing where they are shaving—and when you consider where they are shaving, it makes sense. There's also a difference in the angle of the blade. The blade on a man's razor is angled more sharply because men shave more aggressively. And that's because they're shaving in an unimportant—to men—area, the face. Women are shaving down there where a slip can affect the whole future of the planet.

The shaving creams are the same for men and women; the only difference is the scent. Women don't want to smell like men and vice versa.

Leg shaving is strictly a cultural thing, but it does provide a service. It helps by removing the top layer of dead cells.

Nair—4-Ounce Bottle—$4.48

Imagine if they had this magic cream that you could rub on your legs and—presto!—your leg hair was gone. Uh, they do. It's called Nair or Neet or Surgi-Cream. It's also called a depilatory and it's a big seller in the drugstore. To the tune of $66.4 million in 1996.

How does Nair work? It burns the hair off. Why do you think it stings?

The main ingredient in Nair is the same as the main ingredient in Cool Whip: water! Obviously, it's not the main active ingredient, which is calcium hydroxide, an astringent that's also found in mortar, plaster and cement. One of its primary uses is dehairing hides. So you can have smooth legs, thanks to the same technology that removes hair from pigskins and cowhides so that we don't have shaggy footballs and hairy gloves.

There is another kind of depilatory, one that isn't much discussed. It's facial depilatory and it is a distinct market from the leg versions. And not because the skin on your face is more sensitive. It isn't. The trade magazine *Drug Topics* notes, "Women often feel embarrassed about visible facial hair and would rather not ask store personnel where to find facial depilatories and bleaches." That means druggists have to figure out some conspicuous (easily spotted), yet out-of-the-way (don't want to be seen buying it) place for facial depilatories because Aunt Gert, the one with the mustache, would just as soon have no one know she used facial depilatory. Come to think of it, she didn't use one.

On the positive side, facial depilatories don't have seasonal sales swings. Leg depilatories do because of swimsuit weather.

Revco Calamine Lotion—4-Ounce Bottle—98¢

How many other drugstore products are an integral part of rock and roll history? This one is. The 1959 Coasters song "Poison Ivy" included this legendary line: "Gonna need an ocean/Of calamine lotion." Who else but songwriters Lieber and Stoller would have thought of the visual image of an ocean of calamine lotion? Plus, it rhymes. It's a wonderful rhyme.

Despite the fact that every schoolboy and girl is taught an-

other rhyme—"Leaves in three, leave them be"—poison ivy
continues to be a summertime hazard. I won't detail any poison-
ivy-on-the-privates stories. They would hurt me just to type
them.

Serious cases of poison ivy are no longer treated with
calamine lotion. Would the Coasters song still be a hit? Probably, but the preferred treatment today is hydrocortisone acetate.
But for run-of-the-mill itchy arms and rashy legs, calamine lotion remains the treatment of choice for many parents despite an
FDA ban on advertising calamine lotion as a treatment for poison ivy. Now calamine lotion must be advertised as a "skin pro-
tectant." The FDA says there are no studies proving it is a safe
and effective treatment. No studies, my ass. Did I mention the
study I conducted when I was a kid after taking a dump in the
woods and wiping with poison ivy?

Rogaine Update, Four Months Later:
The Final Chapter

Rogaine is not the answer unless the question is,
How can I spend thirty dollars a month to grow
twenty-eight hairs on my head?

Several chapters and several months ago, I began
my Great Rogaine Adventure, an experiment to see if
the new over-the-counter hair-growth drug would
grow hair on a middle-aged scalp that had been bald
for almost twenty-five years.

Yes, it will. Rogaine grows hair, just not a lot of
hair.

In my four-month Rogaine experiment, I didn't

even grow enough new hairs for a bad comb-over. To be precise, I grew twenty-eight new hairs. (My wife counted.)

At the beginning of the experiment, I had a nice luxurious layer of fuzz on the top of my head. After four months of twice-daily applications, I now have twenty-eight long hairs, plus a nice luxurious layer of fuzz. Most of the new growth is on the top of my head—not the crown, as the Rogaine box predicted, and not the front as I had hoped. There is one new hair in front.

Rogaine is not, as some of its detractors call it, no gain. There is gain, there is new hair.

Was it worth it? Yes, it was worth it to find out if Rogaine would do me any good.

Maybe there's a reason there are no before–after Rogaine ads with a cueball guy on the left and a Lothario-looking bushy head on the right. If Rogaine had worked miracles like that, they would have signed the guy to a Jordanesque contract and still made tons of money.

Rogaine is the first step. It's like they've invented a bad fertilizer. Maybe someday someone will invent a good fertilizer.

Will I continue to use Rogaine? Yes, until the current bottle is empty. But after that, no. It is not worth thirty dollars a month to maintain those twenty-eight new hairs. And that's the downside of Rogaine: When you stop, they go.

But it was worth the effort. It was worth confronting my bald soul, to stare into the mirror at my hairless pate and ask, Do I want hair? How much would it be worth to have hair?

Yes, I'd like hair. But not badly, not desperately. Even if Rogaine had given me Cosmo Kramer hair, I think thirty dollars a month for the rest of my life is a bit steep.

So, for me at least, Rogaine is not the answer. Maybe in another ten years they will have another hair-growth product on the market. And maybe I'll try it. And maybe you'll get to read about it . . .

Ten Things You May Not Know About Rogaine

1. It's a spray, not a cream. So you don't have to rub it in.
2. You have to spray it on twice a day, morning and night.
3. It's not cheap: it's about thirty dollars for a one-month supply.
4. That's three hundred sixty dollars a year, for the mathematically impaired.
5. There is a generic that costs only about thirteen dollars a month.
6. That's still one hundred fifty-six dollars a year.
7. If you stop using it, all your new hair growth will eventually fall out.
8. That is, if you have any new hair growth—not everyone does.
9. It doesn't hurt.
10. It doesn't help.

11

Checking Out:
Maybe for Good

It's no secret that the drugstore checkout counter is covered with "impulse items," things we need but forget we need until we see them. Toilet paper is not an impulse item. It's on the list. But lip balm? Who goes out to get lip balm? Lip balm is one of two perennial checkout counter best-sellers, according to a 1996 survey by the Chain Drug Marketing Association. The other is the emery board.

Razor blades were once a popular checkout counter item, but they have become so popular among the klepto crowd that most drugstores have moved them back into the store. Other checkout counter best-sellers are candy, breath mints, batteries and disposable cameras.

The checkout counter is also a great place to display new items, recent inventions that cause shoppers to pause and ask, "I wonder if that would work." If the item is priced right—under three dollars—it can leap off the counter and into the bag. The top two new items of 1996 were the Isoflex massage ball and IBD's 5-Second Nail Glue.

Scanners started in the supermarkets but now have invaded most every shopping venue going. Though those little UPC symbols are so ubiquitous that we no longer notice them, they've only been around since 1970, and they've only been ubiquitous since the early eighties.

Want to know how to read a drugstore UPC code?

The first number on the left, a lone digit, tells what the category of the item: 3 is for drugs; 0 is for groceries; 2 is for items sold by weight.

Next comes a five-digit cluster that tells the manufacturer: 37000 is Procter & Gamble's manufacturer's code; 35000 belongs to Colgate-Palmolive. Next comes a long center-bar group that tells the scanner, Here comes the product code. The next five numbers identify the product. The same code with a 00359 in front of it could mean a condom instead of a cookie jar, depending on the manufacturer's code preceding it.

The final number, hanging out there on its own, is called the check digit. There is a verification formula in the system that all the other numbers are run through. If the result is not the check digit, then the bar code has been tampered with and you will be arrested immediately by an ancient security guard with an unloaded gun.

Photo Processing

It was a natural fit. Druggists sold chemicals. Photo processing required chemicals. Getting your film developed became as easy as going to the drugstore.

In 1885, *American Druggist* devoted an entire issue to the topic of photography and film processing. Interestingly enough, the article was illustrated not with photos, but with drawings. The anonymous author recommended film processing to druggists: "Due to improvements in photographic processes, which enable one, with no chemical knowledge and little manipulative skill, to produce at least passable pictures."

Many drugstores still offer photo finishing, as it has become known. But it's more a service than a profit center. That's because supermarkets and stand-alone one-hour-developing kiosks have stolen away most of the business.

The drugstore is no longer the place to turn in your film and then wait three days to get those grainy, out-of-focus photos of the ceiling back. They still do a healthy business in film and disposable cameras, selling $777 million worth of film products in 1996.

Fuji DRI-60 Audiotapes, 60 Minutes—2-Pack—$2.99

Audiotapes are one of the top impulse items in the drugstore. That's why they are right next to the cash register, so seductive in their shiny cellophane packaging with all those fancy Dolby words on it. But I would hate to have an audiotape emergency, because tapes are the hardest product in the drugstore to get into, harder even than childproof caps.

You could seriously injure yourself or your high-tech machinery if you don't know what to do. Here's a step-by-step guide to opening the packaging:

1. Remove the cellophane. While it is possible to force the tape—box, cellophane and all—into your tape recorder, it is not desirable. It won't record.

1a. Removing the cellophane is easier said than done. Most brands of tapes have one of those strips that are supposed to peel the plastic off easily. Finding that strip is a challenge worthy of Columbus. You will probably have to find your own starting place on the cellophane. The gathered places on the bottom and sides of the tape, where the cellophane was heat-welded together, look promising but seldom yield happy results.

1b. The best thing to do is to get a sharp kitchen knife—butter knives will only exasperate you—and poke the point into the space where the lid of the tape box meets the bottom.

1c. Once you have plunged the knife into that opening, slide it around, *Psycho*-style, to create a slash in the cellophane.

1d. Now put the knife away, so you won't be tempted to harm the tape when a later step fails.

1e. Try lifting the cellophane slash with your fingernail. If your nail or the slash is long enough, you just may be able to start a run in the cellophane. You may be able to keep the run going all the way to the other end of the tape. Then it is just a matter of peeling off the cellophane.

1f. Most likely this didn't work. Go get the knife again. Slip the flat of the blade into the slash, in the opposite direction you used to create the slash, and then wriggle it around, *Psycho*-style, again. If fortune is on your side, you just may have created a long slash in the cellophane. Now peeling should be no problem.

1g. Most likely you didn't create a long slash. Most likely you just frustrated yourself. Stand up, walk around, shake out your arms, breathe deeply and say three times, "I paid for the tape; the tape is mine."

1h. Search the room for the knife that you threw in anger. Insert the flat of the blade into whatever slash you can find in the cellophane and turn until the blade is perpendicular to the slash. Carefully push the sharp of the blade through the cellophane.

1i. Because heat-sealed cellophane has static electricity in its atomic structure, it will cling more tightly than Saran Wrap. It may appear that you still aren't through the wrapping. You are.

1j. Carefully put the knife away. Using both hands, grab the cellophane on opposite sides of the box and in a single tearing motion, rip the wrapping away. If need be, you may scream, "Aaaaaaiiiiieeeee!" as you do this.

2. Now you must remove the tape from the box. If you are lucky, the box is loose and the tape has already fallen on the floor.

2a. Most likely you aren't lucky and the tape is nestled securely inside the box. And I mean securely.

2b. Insert your fingernail into the space between the top and the bottom of the box and gently lift. If you are lucky, the box lid should spring up and you can shake the tape into your free hand. If instead you feel a tearing sensation in your nail, stop.

2c. Next, try placing your thumbs on the edge of the box and lifting. If you are lucky, the lid will lift up and you should have your tape extracted.

2d. Probably you aren't lucky. Remember that knife we used in steps 1b through 1j? Go get it again.

2e. Slip the knife into the slot between the top and the bottom and gently—GENTLY!—lift. If you are lucky, you should have the tape in one hand and the box in the other.

2f. Unfortunately this seldom works either. Throw the damned box against the wall. If you are lucky, the box will spring open and the tape won't break.

3. If the tape casing breaks, return to the drugstore and buy a new tape.

4. Begin step 1 again.

Magazines

TRUE CONFESSIONS — $1.95
DETECTIVE FILES — $2.50

Lots of folks have drugstore memories like my friend Chris Wohlwend's. "All I remember about the local drugstore was Mr. Hawley yelling at me while I was looking through *Argosy* and *True* for near-naked women pictures. He'd yell, 'Hey son, if you're not going to buy that magazine, put it back. This ain't the library.'"

True and *Argosy.* They were drugstore staples, along with *True Detective, Police Gazette, Radio-TV Mirror, Screen Stories, True Romance, True Confessions* and *Photoplay.*

Where do you think Dad saw his first naked woman? Okay, it was an artist's rendering of a naked woman, in *True* magazine. And he had been prepared for it by *True Detective*, where he saw his first near-naked woman. She was dead, of course. *True Detective* could only publish near-naked photos of dead people.

Call them drugstore magazines. They were the periodicals that filled the racks at the corner drug. *True* and *Argosy* were men's magazines from the Hemingway school: adventure tales mixed in with hunting-and-fishing memoirs. *True Detective* and *Police Gazette* were police procedurals for those with short attention spans.

The movie magazines, *Photoplay* and *Movie Mirror* and the like, were for secretaries on their lunch hour, looking for something to read, to soak up a little reflected glamour of the Hollywood variety. They didn't care about the plots of the new movies; they cared about the stars.

And then there were the confession magazines. Yes, that was once a thriving category of periodicals. Led by *True Confessions* and *Modern Romance*, they have been pushed to the corner now by romance novels. As late as 1975, the top magazines in this category were selling half a million copies a month (down from a million copies a month in the fifties).

What happened to drugstore magazines?

Most of them are gone, victims of changing times and changing tastes.

Photoplay couldn't evolve into *Entertainment Weekly*. Its readers weren't interested in the substance of the latest films or TV shows. *Photoplay* was the *People* of its day, but without the credibility. Secretaries didn't know if the stories were true . . . nor did they care.

In 1970, *Photoplay* had a circulation of more than a million copies a month (1,119,619, to be exact). Today, you can't find a copy of *Photoplay*. It ceased publication in August 1977.

That same year, 1970, *True Confessions* was selling 450,000 copies a month. Today, it sells a little over half that, 280,000 copies a month, according to its editor, Pat Byrdsong.

Yes, *True Confessions* lives, even if you haven't picked up a copy since Ike meant the president, not Tina Turner's ex-husband.

"Our audience hasn't changed much since the fifties and sixties," says Byrdsong. "It's still a magazine targeted largely to women who are blue-collar workers or spouses of blue-collar workers. The cover has changed to keep up with the times. Our cover lines are a little more daring, but the stories are not more daring."

A 1997 issue offers readers such true confessions as "Sex with My Teacher Got Me an 'A'" and "I'm Black, She's White—Will We Ever Be Together?" Scandalous stuff to the casual eye. But read the stories and you will be struck by the purity of the confessions. "Sex with Teacher" also got her pregnant, but it brought her back together with a friend who cared. (I couldn't find the part about getting the A.) Sex exists in a TV-movie style, in another room, out of camera range.

The 1997 *Writer's Market* lists only six magazines in its "Romance and Confession" category. Twenty-five years earlier, Confessions was its own category, and there were twenty-eight entries, from *Confidential Confessions* and *Daring Romances* to *Intimate Secrets* and *Real Story*.

How has *True Confessions* managed to hang on in a world full of chattering Maurys and shouting Geraldos? Byrdsong says the magazine has three keys to its success: "One, we're still using the same concept and it works: women telling other women their stories. This is something that speaks to the heart. Two, we are a continuation of the talk shows. We cover the subjects in a more realistic and honest way. They tend to be exploitative.

We're not. And three, women can find answers to their problems in seeing how other women have handled the problem."

The oldest of the drugstore magazines was *Police Gazette* (technically *National Police Gazette*), which published its first edition in 1845. It was the *Inside Edition* of its day, chasing gruesome murders and lurid romances. By the fifties, the focus had shifted to include gossip. Marilyn Monroe was a regular cover girl because anything connected to her sold. By 1969, circulation—once over a million—was 300,000. It folded in 1974.

But its tradition is carried on today in a handful of detective magazines, all of them published by Globe Communications and all of them edited by Dominick Merle. The newest of Merle's nine detective journals is forty years old. The oldest is eighty-eight.

Detective Files, one of the pups, is forty-one years old and carrying on the tradition of selling issues with near-naked women. A recent cover (May 1997) features a bikini-clad blond cradling an automatic rifle and staring off the cover, under the headline "Nude in the Ice Block."

Merle admits detective magazines are not what they once were. "Our circulation number has dropped since the fifties but appears to have leveled off." He says that the audience is basically the same as it was half a century ago, "the armchair-detective type." It's just that there aren't as many of them buying magazines anymore. Part of the reason for that is TV. "TV has hurt all of publishing to some extent," Merle says. Armchair detectives also have true-crime paperbacks—a category that didn't even exist in the fifties—and reality TV shows to sate this appetite for blood and near-naked women.

And those near-naked women are not what they once were.
They are now pretty much confined to the cover ("Texas Bull
Dyke Axe-Slayer," "The Human Bonfire"). Inside is a mix of
straightforward crime stories interrupted by ads for paranoid
book clubs (offering "Bench-Tested Circuits for Surveillance
and Counter-Surveillance Technicians" and "Protect Your As-
sets: How to Avoid Falling Victim to the Government's Forfei-
ture Laws") and $6.95 police badges.

If you want a near-naked woman photo today you have to
head to the feminine hygiene section and check out the chicks
on the douche packages.

Gibson Greeting Card, Happy Belated Birthday— "Wow! I can't believe it's been a year . . . since I forgot your last birthday."—$2.30

Pharmacists love customers who come in and ask directions to
the greeting card section. They love customers who love to send
greeting cards. They love selling greeting cards. They just love
greeting cards. Oh, sure, part of it is because pharmacists like
making people feel good—and what makes you feel better than
getting a greeting card in the mail? But mostly they like greeting
cards because they offer a 50 percent profit margin. You pay a
buck-fifty. The druggist pockets seventy-five cents.

Thank heaven for birthdays and weddings and graduations
and Mother's Day and Father's Day and St. Patrick's Day and
anniversaries and anniversaries I forgot. There's a card for each
of them.

Who buys the most greeting cards? Women.

Of what age? Older women.

Women aged fifty-five to sixty-four buy an average of fifty-seven greeting cards a year! Druggists like you! They really, really like you!

The drugstore has become a battleground between insurance companies and pharmacists. My best friend from high school just closed his drugstore, a victim, he says, of the HMOs. "I can't make any money because of them."

Another pharmacist friend tells me that when a local health-insurance giant was swallowed by an even larger health-insurance giant, he got a letter from the new company. "They said we're cutting back three percent on what we pay for prescriptions. You've got 8,000 customers on our rolls. Take it or leave it."

It's a story you hear over and over when talking to small-town druggists. The health-insurance giants are trimming here and there and everywhere. One company gives druggists a forty-eight-cent profit per prescription, whether the prescription is three dollars or three hundred dollars.

So who's willing to handle the prescription business? The chain stores. "The big chains are just buying traffic," said my pharmacist friend. "They just want to get people in the store so they'll buy the stuff up front. That's why you have to wait for your prescription when you go in a chain store. They tell their pharmacists to make everyone wait, so they'll buy some other stuff."

It works, this handling prescriptions at cost, or even a loss. "When [a store down the road] dropped out of the Ford and GE insurance plans, their traffic dropped forty-five percent," he said.

That's a recipe for disaster. Because prescriptions that make us feel better, stronger and happier are what drugstores are all about.

The drugstore is an Rx for good health.

Maybe that's the way to wind up our trip through the drugstore, with an explanation for that prescription.

Just what is an Rx?

Rx is short for *recipere,* the Latin word for "take," as in "take this twice a day." In the early days of the drugstore, a prescription would come from a doctor's office. You know all about doctors' handwriting. The doctor would use his med school training—Latin and all that—and write the Latin word for take, *recipere,* at the top. And to the poor pharmacists who had to— and still have to—decipher that scrawl, it looked like "Rx."

And thus the universal shorthand for prescription derives from the fact that doctors have poor penmanship.

At least that's my story, and I'm sticking to it.

Appendix

The Corner Drug Census

The Corner Drug Store
2087 E. Florida Avenue
Hemet, CA 92544

Corner Drug Store
302 Main Street
Seal Beach, CA 90740

Corner Drug Co.
602 Main Street
Woodland, CA 95695

Corner Drug & Hardware
10 S. Main
Driggs, ID 83422

Corner Drug Inc.
7206 Main
Bonners Ferry, ID 83805

Corner Drug Store
2 N. 4th Street
Clear Lake, IA 50428

Corner Drug
201 1st Avenue E.
Dyersville, IA 52040

Corner Drug Store
100 N. Main Street
Sigourney, IA 52591

Corner Drug Store
223 N. Main Street
Bicknell, IN 47512

The Corner Drug Store
530 Main Street
Kiowa, KS 67070

Corner Drug Store
101 N. Public Square
Greensburg, KY 42743

Corner Drug Store
2 N. Main Street
Winchester, NY 40391

Corner Drug Store
424 N. Adams Street
Sturgis, KY 42459

Corner Drug Store
403 S. 19th Street
Baton Rouge, LA 70806

The Corner Drug Store
120 S. Trenton Street
Ruston, LA 71270

Corner Drug Store
1 Minnesota Avenue E.
Glenwood, MN 56334

Corner Drug Store
204 Valley Green Square
Le Sueur, MN 56058

Corner Drug
122 Washburne Avenue
Paynesville, MN 56362

Corner Drug
401 W. 3rd Street
Red Wing, MN 55066

Corner Drug
202 Labree Avenue N.
Thief River Falls, MN 56701

Corner Drug Store
101 W. Railroad Avenue N.
Magnolia, MS 39652

Corner Drug Store
1123 Washington Street
Vicksburg, MS 39180

Corner Drug
1500 E. Main Street
Bethany, MO 64424

The Corner Drugstore
12301 Natural Bridge Road
Bridgeton, MO 63044

Corner Drug Store
308 W. Dallas
Buffalo, MO 65622

Corner Drug Store
102 N. Broadway Street
Bloomfield, NE 68718

Corner Drug Store
201 W. Fox Street
Carlsbad, NM 88220

Corner Drug Store
Main and Washington
Cattaraugus, NY 14719

Corner Drug Store
101 W. Main Street
Endicott, NY 13760

The Corner Drug Store
451 3rd Avenue
New York, NY 10016

Corner Drug Store
Main Street
South Fallsburg, NY 12779

Corner Drug Store
522 Dakota Avenue
Wahpeton, NJ 58075

Corner Drug
1005 W. Main Street
Durant, OK 74701

Corner Drug Store
100 W. Lillie Boulevard
Madill, OK 73446

Corner Drug Store
326 N. 6th Street
Perry, OK 73077

The Corner Drug Store
205 W. Cedar Rock Street
Pickens, SC 29671

Corner Drug Company
414 S. Main Avenue
Lake City, TN 37769

Corner Drug Store
640 Tri County Boulevard E.
Oliver Springs, TN 37840

Corner Drug
200 N. Main Street
Andrews, TX 79714

Corner Drug
539 Spring Street
Columbus, TX 78934

Corner Drug
101 E. Main Street
Llano, TX 78643

Corner Drug
122 S. Main Street
Perryton, TX 79070

Corner Drug Store
222 Main Street
Quanah, TX 79252

Corner Drug
122 N. Main Street
Shamrock, TX 79079

Corner Drug Co. Inc.
27 Maple Street
White River Junction,
   VT 05001

Corner Drug Store
239 N. Main Street
Blacksburg, VA 24060

Corner Drug Store
255 E. Main Street
Pullman, WA 99163

Corner Drug Store
100 W. 3rd Street
Baraboo, WI 53913

Corner Drug Store
206 S. Iowa Street
Dodgeville, WI 53533

Corner Drug
300 W. Main Street
Lander, WY 82520